SUDDENLY

JOHN
BETTY

**LEARNING TO START
OVER THROUGH THE
EXPERIENCE OF OTHERS**

SIMON AND

SINGLE

ROBERTSON
UTTERBACK

Foreword by
SALLY JESSY RAPHAEL

SCHUSTER   New York

We would like to dedicate this book to:
Barbara
Max
Dot
Joe

COPYRIGHT © 1986 BY JOHN ROBERTSON
ALL RIGHTS RESERVED
INCLUDING THE RIGHT OF REPRODUCTION
IN WHOLE OR IN PART IN ANY FORM
PUBLISHED BY SIMON AND SCHUSTER
A DIVISION OF SIMON & SCHUSTER, INC.
SIMON & SCHUSTER BUILDING
ROCKEFELLER CENTER
1230 AVENUE OF THE AMERICAS
NEW YORK, NEW YORK 10020
SIMON AND SCHUSTER AND COLOPHON ARE REGISTERED TRADEMARKS
OF SIMON & SCHUSTER, INC.
DESIGNED BY KAROLINA HARRIS
MANUFACTURED IN THE UNITED STATES OF AMERICA
10 9 8 7 6 5 4 3 2 1

LIBRARY OF CONGRESS CATALOGING IN PUBLICATION DATA
Robertson, John, DATE–
   Suddenly single.

   Bibliography: p.
   1. Divorced people–United States–Psychology.
2. Widows–United States–Psychology.   3. Widowers–
United States–Psychology.   4. Separation (Psychology)
5. Grief.   I. Utterback, Betty.   II. Title.
HQ834.R58   1986   306.8′8   85-27889
ISBN: 0-671-54442-X

CONTENTS

FOREWORD BY SALLY JESSY RAPHAEL		6
INTRODUCTION		9
One	SHOCK	15
Two	REACTIONS TO SHOCK	35
Three	THE LEGAL ASPECTS	56
Four	THE DYING MARRIAGE	80
Five	SOCIALLY SINGLE	98
Six	LIFE CHANGES	122
Seven	THE EMOTIONAL RECOVERY	145
Eight	THE OLDER SINGLE	171
Nine	REJOINING THE WORLD	193
EPILOGUE		211
FOR FURTHER READING		217

FOREWORD

Dealing with a loss—a divorce, the death of a partner, or a broken relationship—can be horrendous. In fact, you can be a victim of life instead of one of its winners. I believe this book will lead you to understand loss, to work through it and to achieve new levels of fulfillment and serenity.

In *Suddenly Single,* we follow the lives of eight people who share their stories and the suffering they have endured while under the tremendous stress of sudden personal loss. Follow Sara's recovery from a sudden divorce as she learns to cope daily with her new life and new identity. Learn how Laura, following the death of her husband, becomes comfortable with her newly developed poise and regained self-confidence. Read how Richard, who lost Peggy and had to raise their children himself, learns to stop thinking he has to be two parents in one and how he comes to share his plans and goals with others, without the fear of being judged. A divorce can be catastrophic for some who, like Frank, after being divorced from Jill, leaps into the first relationship that comes along and then quickly divorces again. We hear from Frank how he learns to live with himself after working through the second loss. He is now on the firm road to recovery.

John Robertson and Betty Utterback, using these and other case histories, and in addition, the expert opinions of the professionals they quote, convey to the reader that those who find themselves suddenly single are not alone or unique in their experiences—many others out there have suffered and worked through what the authors pinpoint as the "five steps of a loss."

Sometimes the grieving process causes victims to jump foolishly into the first relationship that comes along to prove to themselves that they are still alive and functioning human beings. A casual sexual relationship . . . an identity crisis . . . a stab in the dark to find out who and what they are . . . a search for belonging. Divorce or death of a person's mate frequently disrupts the ability to function on the upper plane of life and forces one to regress, to become concerned about fulfilling only the most basic need—survival.

Robertson and Utterback note: "The trauma of becoming 'suddenly single' is a personal experience. The feeling of being abandoned, of total isolation, overwhelms everything else for a time. Friendships appear shallow, close relatives may appear heartless and even one's children may temporarily be forgotten. Despair may obliterate simple pleasures."

During the four years that I have been on NBC's *Talknet*, the topic of loss, whether through divorce or death, has come up at least once a night and sometimes the entire program focuses on this issue. Of those who share their intimate stories in this book, the more successful show that the task of reordering their shattered lives is not only possible, but worth the effort, however long it takes. These victims of sudden loss now believe that if they had only known then that their feelings were normal and that there was hope, their burden would have been lighter and their recovery process briefer.

The suffering that some feel when confronted with a sudden loss is sometimes so great that they become overwhelmed by the thought that life simply cannot go on. The effort of working through the trauma and stress of the loss—the effort of returning to normalcy—is more than some can bear. I only hope and pray that this book will be available to anyone who suffers.

Guiding those who have suffered is not an easy task. The key lies in opening up the mind, to allow it to return to normal. The greatest challenge is to live one's life to the fullest. In today's hectic world, the task of being an individual—even if one is married—must be a goal for all of us. We must stand as individuals, work through the enormous stress of losing a partner . . . and at the same time realize that we cannot do it alone. Using this book as a guideline, the reader will be touched by all of the intimate stories that are shared by the authors. The best recourse is to ask for help, listen to serious friends and responsible people . . . trust our instincts . . . and get on with our lives.

Sally Jessy Raphael
December 1985

INTRODUCTION

The idea for *Suddenly Single,* sparked by a personal experience, resurfaced persistently over a period of more than two years before we finally agreed the book should be written.

Two members of John's immediate family had become suddenly single, one through legal separation and the other by death. As commonplace as both events appeared, John became aware of the dramatic adjustments each of his close relatives had to make and the unexpected rippling effect on their families.

Having worked together previously on a writing project, we began to explore the possibilities of a book on the problems of the suddenly single.

During our preliminary research, we became acutely aware of the magnitude and diversity of the subject. The statistical evidence alone was mind-boggling, indicating that virtually everyone is touched by the problem in one way or another at some point in their lives. Attempting to focus on the subject in any meaningful way loomed as a monumental task. We abandoned the project for more than a year.

Looking back, we may have become overly sensitized. The

subject of death and divorce seemed to crop up everywhere. We listened with heightened awareness to the personal stories of friends and acquaintances who were going through traumatic adjustments, often with little help or support. In many cases, they were chastising themselves for not living up to some preconceived notion of how the suddenly single person should react and behave.

As part of the preliminary research, a marriage therapist in private practice had recruited for us several volunteer subjects willing to be interviewed. These people were sincere and unselfish, ready to take off their happy masks and let down the barriers on the chance that their stories might help others. Clearly, these people were hurting.

Ultimately, the cumulative impact of their personal stories convinced us we should find some way to present them effectively in book form. We agreed that the focus of the book must be on the hurt, the sense of vulnerability these people were feeling.

In order to broaden our cross section of subjects and lifestyles, John contacted friends in various parts of the country, many of whom also agreed to be interviewed, in the course of either personal visits or lengthy telephone conversations. Many followed up with detailed written reports on their progress. Others shared pertinent letters and diaries. Betty started writing detailed case histories on each of the subjects. Although both of us conducted interviews, some of them jointly, we wrote them in the first person for the sake of continuity, using assumed names in most cases for considerations of privacy.

We found the subjects surprisingly open and willing to answer even the most intimate questions, invariably expressing the hope that we would "tell it like it is."

We were further surprised by the numbers. Eventually, as people learned we were working on the project, everyone we came into contact with seemed to have a story or to know someone who might be willing to tell us about their experiences. One unusual example is a waitress who served us at a dinner meeting one evening. She was obviously curious about our conversation, about the manuscript and the notes spread out on the table, so we asked her if she had ever been divorced or widowed. She told us her story, serving it in courses along with the meal. It, too, became part of the data that reinforced the information in our case histories.

By the end of the first year, Betty had incorporated approximately thirty of the case histories into the first draft of the book. The number made the stories difficult to follow, yet each represented some facet of the adjustment process that we were reluctant to delete. Our editor, Don Hutter, came to the rescue by suggesting that some of the case histories could be woven into composite subjects without losing the reality we wanted to retain. This technique improved both the clarity and continuity of the book.

We asked several recently divorced and widowed persons to read the second draft of the manuscript. They assured us, often through tears, "Yes, that's how it is."

We had apparently accomplished our initial goal—to let the suddenly single know they are not alone or unique in their responses. Then we realized this was not enough. If many were as traumatized by their experience as we now believed, they would need more specific advice than our chapter summaries provided. They would need to know how the positive and negative experiences described in the case histories could be applied to their own lives.

Our editor suggested expanding the analysis sections and incorporating them into the text of the book. This meant months of additional work and, again, turning to the professionals for more information.

The final draft bore little resemblance to our initial outline. As we followed our subjects through to recovery, they seemed to take over and give the book a life of its own. We could not have predicted, for example, that Sara Johnston would find a totally new, rewarding life.

The subjects often surprised us even in small ways, making it constantly necessary to adjust and reform the book. When Frank Gardener spoke of using his journals as an outlet for anger, for example, we assumed the journals would be filled with angry words. This was not the case. When he located the journals he had kept during that period, the entries reflected his tentative, almost gentle frame of mind through his crisis. His generosity in sharing the actual journals gave his story a reality we could not have achieved otherwise.

In the end, the book belonged to the subjects. We had become the conduits.

We are grateful to a number of people who helped and supported our efforts along the way.

Dr. Dennis Boike, a private therapist in Rochester, New York, deserves special recognition for his ongoing support and professional advice during the final months of work. Dr. Boike and his staff of six mental health professionals have become well known in the upstate New York area for their team approach in working with the divorced and bereaved. Despite his busy schedule, Dr. Boike spent many hours going over each of the case histories, offering invaluable psychological insight. He was always available when questions arose, often late at night.

Family and marriage counselor Susan Horwitz read the manuscript in the early stages and again before the final draft, making numerous helpful comments. Formerly in private practice, Horwitz is a therapist on the staff of the Family & Marriage Clinic at the University of Rochester Medical Center.

Psychologist John Connally, a specialist in hypnosis and behavioral medicine in private practice, was particularly helpful in explaining the symptoms and treatment of Sara Johnston's agoraphobia. Recognized for his work with phobic patients, Connally has recently worked with dentists on the treatment of dental phobia.

Divorce lawyer Richard Williams, a member of the law firm of Kaman, Berlove, Marafioti, Jacobstein & Goldman, went over the legal chapter, offering advice and comments.

Ruth Jean Loewinsohn, of the Widowed Persons Service, American Association of Retired Persons, read the manuscript before the final draft and provided helpful advice on issues concerning the widowed. Loewinsohn is an experienced counselor and author of *Survival Handbook for Widows*.

Finally, Don Hutter, in addition to providing helpful advice in progress, edited the final draft of the book with a sensitive pen.

We hope the result of all our efforts will be useful to those who find themselves suddenly single.

—John Robertson and Betty Utterback

"Problems do not go away. They must be worked through or else they remain, forever a barrier to the growth and development of the spirit."

—M. Scott Peck,
The Road Less Traveled

1: SHOCK

Sara Johnston awoke before dawn with the uneasy premonition that something bad was about to happen. Then, abruptly awake from a deep, pill-induced sleep, she remembered. The bad thing had already happened.

Sara's husband, Jim, had moved out of the house the evening before, and for the first time, she was alone. The silence! Sara switched on the bedside light and fumbled for her house slippers.

As she stood up, a sensation of vertigo swept over her. The familiar walls of her bedroom seemed to sway around her. Her heart pounded. She gasped for breath.

I'm going to faint, Sara thought. Will anyone find me?

And then the most frightening thought surfaced. Will anyone *want* to find me?

Carefully, bolstering all her strength, Sara put one foot in front of the other. The sensation of dizziness finally passed as she reached the bathroom. She peered at her face in the bathroom mirror and saw a stranger.

"I must be losing my mind," she whispered.

A petite, pretty woman of forty-seven, Sara put up a brave

front when her husband of twenty-six years suddenly walked out on her. But, she said, "I was slowly crumbling inside."

Like many women of her generation, Sara had invested everything in her marriage. Whatever disappointments she may have experienced through the years, the marriage had held the promise of lifelong security. She felt stunned, betrayed.

Although divorce represents a crisis in anyone's life, the impact can be devastating on women like Sara who have relied on the marriage for companionship, financial support, even personal identity over a long period of time. Sara had been married more than half her life.

Sara had agreed to an interview, and at her suggestion, we met at a small French restaurant in New York City to save me the drive to her home in Connecticut. It was still early for the dinner crowd, and the headwaiter led us to a small table in a quiet alcove.

"Dubonnet and soda," Sara told the waiter, barely glancing at him.

I ordered a glass of white wine and we fell into small talk about the weather and the scarcity of taxis. I placed my notebook and ballpoint pen on the table, wondering if Sara was comfortable enough to begin.

"I was planning a little dinner party for our twenty-sixth anniversary when Jim told me," Sara said suddenly as if reading my thoughts. "He had to find himself, he said."

Smiling slightly, she added, "I think it was just a polite way of saying he wants to sleep with younger women."

With her stylishly coiffed reddish-brown hair, Sara had the look of a woman who had taken care of herself. Her outfit, a paisley skirt and natural silk blazer, was neat and well tailored. A miniature gold golf club with a diamond imbedded in it dangled from a gold chain around her neck. Sara certainly hadn't lost her husband by "letting herself go."

She looked at me questioningly after the waiter had served

our drinks. "Why is it men seem to get more interesting as they grow older, women just grow older?"

Sara and Jim had met when they were both students at Indiana University. After getting her degree in nursing, Sara had worked for a year in a Bloomington, Indiana, hospital while Jim finished his last year of dental school.

"I didn't think of my job as a career," Sara said. "My goal in life was to get married and have a family. That wasn't at all unusual in those days. I think most of my friends felt the same way."

Sara had continued to work after Jim's graduation. They had gone through a lean year while Jim struggled to establish himself in the small city of New London, Connecticut. Having taken over a practice from a retiring dentist, Jim had made a major investment in new equipment and initially lost some patients who couldn't adjust to the change. Within two years, however, he had built up his own following of patients and had begun to show a profit.

The timing was perfect. Sara was pregnant and she couldn't wait to become a full-time housewife and mother. She quit her job when she was six months pregnant and glowed with happiness at the surprise baby shower her coworkers gave on her last day. She had saved the crepe paper stork favor for her baby's scrapbook.

A good nurse, Sara had become a supermother. Always the first on the block to volunteer, she had become the perennial den mother, P.T.A. leader, and Sunday school teacher.

Contentedly immersed in domestic life, she had enjoyed the material rewards of her husband's success, including the move to the 150-year-old saltbox-style house where she now lived alone.

"I always thought of Jim's success as our success, and I'm sure he felt the same at one time," Sara said. "Even when he started spending a lot of evenings and weekends out on our boat, I thought he was just being a kid enjoying his new toy.

I'm not a sailing enthusiast, and frankly, I was grateful he didn't insist on my always going along."

One summer evening, after pouring martinis into chilled glasses before dinner, Jim told Sara he had to leave her.

"I felt like I'd just dropped ten stories in a broken elevator. He didn't say he wanted to leave. He said he *had* to leave. There was something so final about that."

Jim informed Sara that he planned to give up his dental practice and open a marina. His work had become boring and unfulfilling.

I had a sudden, vivid image of Jim getting his hair styled, opening his shirt to the navel, and dangling gold chains around his neck in a frantic attempt to recapture his youth. The mental image of a man in the throes of a midlife crisis was, perhaps, simplistic and possibly unfair, but at the moment, it was hard to empathize with the person apparently responsible for the obvious pain in Sara's face.

Despite that pain, Sara had some things going for her. Unlike many women who are abandoned at midlife with no means of support, Sara had a part-time job. Shortly after their youngest child had gone away to college, Sara had become restless with her volunteer work and started working twenty hours a week in the administrative office of the hospital.

"I would have described myself as a fairly independent person," Sara said, thoughtfully sipping her drink. "But when Jim left, I felt lost, rudderless."

The anxiety attacks continued. Waking up with a start as early as three A.M., Sara would sit at the kitchen table drinking coffee and smoking.

"Somehow, I always managed to get myself together in time to go to work. It seemed to take all my strength to get through those four hours in the morning. Except for going to work, I rarely went out."

A brief entry in Sara's diary would later provide her with an important clue:

Today I walked over to the little grocery store in the neighborhood to get some milk. While I was standing in the checkout line, I thought I was going to have a heart attack. My heart was pounding and I couldn't breathe. I had to get out of the store, but my legs felt so wobbly I could hardly walk home. I had to concentrate on just going a block at a time. I'm sure there's something physically wrong with me, but I've made three appointments with the doctor and canceled them all. I can't seem to do anything. I don't know why.

Sara's married daughter, who lives in Darien, Connecticut, and her son, who lives in New York City, visited her often during her first weeks alone.

"They praised me for taking it so well and that pleased me," Sara said. "I was not taking it well. I was ashamed of myself for being so weak."

Weak?

Overwhelmed, immobilized, perhaps, but not weak.

"Sara's behavior was perfectly normal for the circumstances," Dr. Dennis Boike said after hearing the details of Sara's story. "She's an almost classic example of a marriage partner who has sacrificed her personal identity for the marital identity. When a separation occurs, all sense of self is fragmented, all semblance of independence lost. I hear her story every day in my office."

Sara's anxiety attacks and extreme insecurity were normal symptoms of separation anxiety. "I call it normal neurosis," said Dr. Boike. "That is, behavior, thoughts, and emotions which would be considered abnormal and neurotic under normal circumstances are quite normal under extreme stress.

"Often the guilt and compulsive behaviors are most acute for the person who's had earlier hints of trouble but refused to face what was observed or sensed."

Sara had, in fact, rationalized Jim's reasons for spending his evenings and weekends on their boat. Her comment that she considered herself a fairly independent person was typical of someone occupationally independent suddenly made aware of how relationally dependent they've been.

"I see this among men as well as women," Dr. Boike noted. "By the way, Sara's panic attack in the grocery store wasn't as strange or unusual as you might think. Haven't you ever wondered about those abandoned grocery carts with the carton of melting ice cream? I've wondered if supermarkets figure divorced people into their overhead."

Sara was in the habit of setting herself up for failure, Dr. Boike pointed out, citing such comments of hers as "Women just get older," and "I never thought of my job as a career." And at a time when she was badly in need of loving support, she had turned away from those closest to her. Her adult children, for example, had made the effort to spend time with her, clearly indicating they wanted to help.

Instead of talking about her feelings and releasing some of her pain, Sara chose to "bear up," to put on a flimsy façade of bravado and strength. It was the same with many of the divorced and widowed who instinctively put on a happy face. Then gradually, almost reluctantly, they would begin to share their personal agony and private tears.

We do it because society seems to admire the stoic, observes Ann S. Kliman in her book, *Crisis*. We're comfortable in sharing positive feelings, hesitant when we feel frightened, angry, needy, or tearful.

Kliman, a clinical psychologist who has worked with individuals and families immediately following a severe personal tragedy, writes: "We feel belittled at these times and don't want others to know, as if such human reactions to severe stress should be alien to us, or on the assumption that the only allowable part of being human is the noble part."

THE PRESSURE ON MEN

The social pressure to bear up and move on after the loss of one's mate has traditionally been even greater on men.

Richard Morrison recalled the summer morning he woke up with a start on the living room couch. He had fallen asleep in front of the television set the night before, and now it was almost seven A.M.

"Dammit, I'm going to be late for work," he muttered, hurrying into the bathroom and turning on the shower.

"Peggy," he yelled to his wife. "Get up."

When she didn't respond, Richard shouted her name angrily as he banged open the door to their bedroom.

He stopped, frozen.

"No," he gasped, rushing to the bed.

Peggy lay sprawled on their bed, dead of a heart attack at age thirty-two.

"It was just like that," Richard said, snapping his fingers. "She had no history of heart problems or illness of any kind. For a while, I couldn't believe the doctors were telling me the truth."

An insurance agent in his mid-thirties, Richard lived in a small tract house on the outskirts of Dansville, Illinois. A muscular man of five feet ten, Richard opened the door to me and apologized for his paint-spattered jeans and the well-worn blue work shirt rolled back to the elbows. Saturday was housework day.

Richard's six-year-old son, Jason, was a miniature version of his dad except for a mop of curly red hair. After a shy "Hello," the little boy went outside to play. The rhythmic thump of a ball bouncing on the blacktop driveway could soon be heard.

"I remember dialing the emergency number for the ambulance," Richard said, running his hand through his prematurely thinning brown hair. "The next thing I knew, the house was filled with people and everyone was asking me questions. It must have been afternoon before they finally took her body away and the police left. Then it finally hit me, I hadn't even thought about the children."

The woman next door, a close friend of Peggy's, had quietly taken charge of the two children, attempting to distract them from the drama taking place at their home—the flashing lights of the police cars and ambulance, the milling crowd of curious neighbors. She had fed them, taken them into her home for the night, and, on the morning of the funeral, helped them get dressed in their best clothes.

Richard had concentrated on making the arrangements for the funeral, a duty he had never been called upon to perform before. There was a sense of unreality about choosing the casket and deciding on the outfit Peggy was to be dressed in. The funeral director, speaking in a soft monotone, kept referring to "the laying out of the body."

Richard tried to recall the significant events of Peggy's life for the obituary. He tried to concentrate when their minister questioned him about the hymns and scriptures he might like to have included in the funeral service.

"The hardest part was calling Peggy's parents and breaking the news to them," Richard said. "I know I must have sounded cold, but I thought I should behave as normally as possible. It's the macho thing. A man's supposed to be strong."

Richard had gone through the ritual of the wake and the funeral dry-eyed and expressionless. Peggy's parents had arrived from Iowa the day after Peggy died and had insisted on staying in a motel. Hardworking farm people, the Parkers lived and had raised their daughter by the strict fundamental rules of the Bible. Richard had always felt uncomfortable around them, taking their silence as a sign that they didn't quite approve of him.

Mr. Parker, dressed in a blue serge suit, looked smaller than Richard remembered him. Peggy's mother, wearing her good black dress with a cameo pin at the throat, was pale and expressionless. Covering her best dress with a big apron she had brought from home, Mrs. Parker had prepared the meals from the bounty of food brought in by the neighbors.

The Parkers had stood beside Richard at the funeral home during the calling hours, but even in their shared grief Richard had realized he had not felt close to them.

"Your mommy has gone to heaven," Mrs. Parker had told the children when they'd returned to the quiet house after the funeral and the brief service at the cemetery. "God decided it was time to take her and she's with Him now."

Richard had wondered if the explanation made any sense to the children. He had wanted to believe that Peggy was with God in heaven, but he couldn't picture it. And why would God want to take her away when her family needed her? None of it made any sense to him.

"You're holding up well," Mr. Parker had said, giving Richard an awkward pat on the shoulder and getting into his car for the long drive back to Iowa.

Richard appeared to be holding up well. His neighbors remarked on what a great job he was doing with the kids and managing all the extra work he had to do.

Never having cooked or helped with the housework while Peggy was alive, Richard had taken charge, getting up early every morning to cook breakfast for the children—Jason, then four, and Amanda, nine—and get Mandy off to school. He had enrolled Jason in a prekindergarten program and dropped him off there on his way to work. He had made arrangements with his office manager to leave work at a set time each day so that he could pick Jason up at the school. The other salesmen in the agency had offered to cover for him in the evening.

Like a man possessed, Richard had thrown himself into his new role. He cooked a full dinner every evening, rejecting the children's suggestions of hot dogs or pizza. He took the time to help Mandy with her homework after dinner and to read Jason a bedtime story. He did the grocery shopping, cleaned the house, and did the laundry on weekends. Everyone who knew him had to agree he was doing a remarkable job.

"One thing I couldn't bring myself to do was talk to the children about their mother," Richard said. "Mandy started acting like a little mother. Jason cried over everything and started sucking his thumb."

About a month after Peggy's death, Jason had looked up from the bowl of oatmeal he had been dabbling in.

"What happened to Mommy?"

Richard had shaken his head helplessly and hurried into the bathroom. Trembling uncontrollably, he had turned the lock.

"The most important thing I learned was that men can cry," Richard said. "I cried a lot after that."

Richard and Peggy had grown up in the same Iowa farming community and attended the same small school. A year older than Peggy, Richard was a year ahead of her in school. They had started pairing off at parties long before Peggy's parents would permit her to date. By the time Peggy was a sophomore and Richard was a junior in high school, they were going steady, taking it for granted that they would eventually get married.

The wedding date had actually been set for a month after Peggy's graduation as the result of circumstances rather than planning. The family doctor who had delivered her and nursed her through childhood diseases had confirmed she was pregnant. Peggy had been horrified by the thought of breaking the news to her parents. Instead, Richard had braced himself for the worst and asked Peggy's father for permission to marry her. To their relief, Peggy's parents had given the marriage their blessing and had never questioned the young couple's haste. Peggy's condition, barely noticeable in her wedding gown, had caused only a slight ripple of gossip in the small farming community.

"I had to give up college and get a job," Richard said. "I didn't mind too much at the time. I'd thought a lot about becoming a teacher, but I was beginning to wonder if I was really cut out for it. Quitting school gave me an out, but I never admitted that to Peggy. Later, when things weren't going so well, I'd always throw that up to her—like it was her fault if I was a failure."

A job offer with an insurance agency in Dansville had seemed like a golden opportunity to get away from their families and strike out on their own. Richard had thrown himself into the new job, spending most of his evenings with prospective clients. Peggy had felt lonely and isolated in the new community. She had trouble keeping up with the baby's demands, trying to keep the house clean, and having dinner ready promptly so that Richard could go out again to keep his evening appointments. Peggy and Richard had begun to pick at each other over trivial things.

"About a year before she died, we'd talked about a separation," Richard said. "I've felt guilty as hell about some of the things I said to her. We couldn't seem to sit down and talk about what was really on our minds, so we'd needle each other—like poking a sore place."

After Peggy died, Richard was haunted by guilt. "If only," he kept saying to himself in the middle of the night as he lay sleepless, staring into the darkness.

Dr. Boike repeats Richard's words: "It finally hit me, I hadn't even thought about the children."

The reaction is typical, says Dr. Boike, explaining, "While in the shock stage, it's normal to be so obsessed with contemplating one's own injured navel that one cannot see another's hurts. Children particularly are neglected, often by otherwise excellent parents."

Mandy tried to become a "little mother" in an effort to maintain a semblance of an intact family. Jason, the younger child, unconsciously tried to get his father's attention by regressing to a baby stage, when he had been nurtured and cared for.

"Both are painful but normal responses to the tragedy they experienced," Dr. Boike says. "Adults tend to forget, it's the kids' event, too."

As long as he continued to shut out his children emotionally and to deny his own feelings by engaging in frenetic activity, Richard would remain stuck in a state of shock.

A NONTRADITIONAL LOVE TRIANGLE

As painful as the death of one's mate may be, we know that death is inevitable. As devastating as the breakup of a marriage can be, divorce has become almost commonplace. But the recent, more open acceptance of gay and lesbian relationships has resulted in broken marriages that can be both painful and confusing.

Carol Dwyer recalled the holiday party she and her husband, Bob Rossiter, and their business partner, Paul Roche, had thrown at the Drake Hotel in Chicago to celebrate their first year in the public relations business.

"I bought the brightest and most expensive dress I could find," Carol said. "It was cherry-red satin. I was on top of the world and I wanted to let everyone know it that night."

Both Bob and Carol were ambitious, prepared to plan long-range goals, and willing to take the risks necessary to achieve them.

After ten years in the public relations department of a major corporation based in Stamford, Connecticut, Bob had decided it was time to make his move and open his own business. He was thirty-five. He had gained valuable experience with the company and taken pains to establish solid business contacts with the decision makers in other companies around the country.

The timing was also right for Carol to make a career change. Having gained local recognition and valuable experience as an artist for an advertising agency, Carol was eager to take on more creative and ambitious projects. She and Bob agreed that the meshing of their talents was ideally suited to starting their own company, and Paul Roche, a friend of Bob's from Chicago, seemed like the ideal choice for a business partner. As a free-lance public relations man, Paul not only had more experience in dealing with individual clients, but he was willing to invest half the capital for start-up costs. Paul was in his mid-forties and ready for something more settled and secure than free-lancing.

"We gave ourselves two years to get the company going," Carol said. "By the end of the first year, we were showing a profit. We had every reason to celebrate."

Carol moved gracefully among the guests, well aware of the admiring glances being cast her way. Her red satin dress accentuated the lithe lines of her tall, slender body, her pale skin, and her shiny black hair caught up in a smooth chignon.

Across the room, Bob was dispensing his charm to a small circle of people, including a sleepy-looking blond woman who appeared to be hanging on his every word.

When Bob glanced her way, Carol smiled and lifted her champagne glass slightly in a private toast. The party was a celebration, but they were also using it to promote their work. They had invited not only their regular clients, but prospective clients as well. Carol felt giddy with excitement and champagne. The long hours, the dedication, were finally paying off even more quickly than they had dared hope.

Carol wasn't sure how it happened. A businessman from

Winnetka was entertaining her with stories about a recent ski trip to Colorado. Suddenly he lunged forward, bumped by someone from behind, and his half-filled glass of champagne splashed over the front of her holiday dress.

Brushing off the man's profuse apologies, Carol looked around the room for Bob. When she couldn't find him, she left the room quickly; she didn't want to show her annoyance.

They had reserved a suite where their out-of-town guests could change or catch a quick rest. Carol found a key in her purse and took the elevator upstairs.

She had no forewarning as she turned the key in the lock and reached for the light switch. As the room was flooded with light, two figures sprang from the bed.

"Oh, God," Bob groaned, coming toward her.

Behind him, hastily grabbing his clothes, was Paul Roche. Carol screamed.

"I think I could have dealt with another woman," Carol said a few months later at the farmhouse she and Bob owned in Bucks County, Pennsylvania. Outside the kitchen window, forsythia bloomed and crocuses dotted the new, pale green grass.

"Maybe I'm naive, but I never suspected anything," Carol said, tracing the rim of her coffee cup with a slender forefinger. "Maybe I just didn't want to."

Carol's classically beautiful face, with her pale skin and high cheekbones, seemed almost gaunt. Her dark, deep-set eyes looked hollow.

"Sex was never important in our marriage," Carol said after a long, thoughtful pause. "When Bob and I first started dating, I admired him for not grabbing me like most of the men I'd dated. I was puzzled when he still didn't show much interest after we were married, but after a while, I just accepted it. We had a lot in common, a lot going for us. We enjoyed the same things. You can't expect to have everything."

With both of them independent and career-oriented, Carol

and Bob had concentrated their energy on work and a social life with other young couples they met through their work.

After they moved to Chicago and started the business, work became their whole life and Paul became part of the family.

"Paul was always around," Carol said. "But we all agreed we couldn't make a go of it unless we really worked at it. Why would I suspect anything?"

Carol and Bob had fought angrily that night after Carol discovered Bob and Paul in their room. Exhausted and slightly drunk on champagne, Carol had finally fallen asleep. When she awoke, Bob was still sitting on the adjoining twin bed with his head in his hands.

"Maybe we ought to talk about it," Carol said finally, drawing her knees up under her chin. She looked at Bob for a time before she could say the words, "Are you homosexual?"

Bob ran his hands through his thick dark hair and shook his head helplessly. "I don't know what I am," he said, sighing heavily. "All I know is, I've been fighting this thing for as long as I can remember. Back in school when the other guys started talking about girls, I knew I wasn't having those feelings.

"I'd try to fake it. Lord, how I faked it. I was on the basketball team and I always went after the most popular girls. It was easy because it was a status thing with them—to date a guy who was good in sports."

Carol pulled her knees closer under her chin. She felt small and defenseless. "How did you feel about boys?" Her words were careful, measured.

"I'd get these weird feelings sometimes and I knew it wasn't right by other people's standards," Bob said. "I'd deny how I felt and try harder than ever to put across that macho image. One night I made it with a hot little cheerleader who threw her body all over me. I thought everything was all right."

"Was it ever all right with me?"

Bob looked at her, tears welling up in his eyes. "There's

one thing you've got to understand, Carol. This has nothing to do with you. It's me. It's my problem. I love you. I'd never intentionally do anything to hurt you."

Carol shook her head. Suddenly she got out of bed and walked across the room, shakily lighting a cigarette.

"How can you possibly say that?" She turned toward him accusingly. "You married me, didn't you?"

Bob nodded, sighing again. "You've got to believe me. I didn't know for sure. I'd never had a homosexual relationship when we got married. I didn't want it to be true. When I met Paul, I couldn't deny it anymore. In a way I hated it, but in another crazy way I was relieved because I could finally be myself."

Carol stubbed out the cigarette.

"If you expect me to understand, I can't," she said, turning her back to him. "I thought we had a good marriage. Now you're telling me it was all a lie."

She turned and looked at her husband as if confronting a stranger.

"You can have anything you want," Bob said helplessly. "Just tell me what you want."

Carol shook her head. "I don't want anything."

After a while, Carol went over to the closet to get her clothes. The bright red dress was hanging there. She pulled it off the hanger and threw it on the floor.

She dressed quickly and went out, walking the streets in a daze, unaware of the crowds brushing by her. Later she wouldn't be able to remember where she had walked or for how long. When she got back, she found a note from Bob propped on the dresser.

"I'm sorry."

"If only it had been another woman, I could have handled it," Carol said.

"If only." It's an expression almost everyone uses to deny the reality of pain.

"If only she [or he] hadn't died so suddenly, it might have been easier," the widowed person says.

"If only he hadn't left me for such a tramp, maybe I could have accepted it," declares the divorced woman.

"If only . . ."

Separation shock can be so intense, we all want to believe we could have handled our personal crisis better "if" the circumstances had been a little bit different.

But, as Dr. Boike expresses it, "Growth can't begin until the person can honestly say, 'I hurt,' and feel the pain."

WHEN DEATH SEVERS A LONG, HAPPY MARRIAGE

Happy marriages do exist. Laura and David Cunningham would have said they were happily married after twenty-five years together. To the Cunninghams happiness meant a general feeling of pleasure and contentment with their life-style. They enjoyed their shared interests and respected each other's differences. They could communicate openly most of the time without inflicting fatal wounds. Above all, they considered themselves good friends.

As an added bonus, they liked their two adult children, who had miraculously survived a rebellious period during the 1960s. While some of his contemporaries had cooked their brains on drugs, their son, Jeff, had gone backpacking around Europe after graduation. He'd come back with a greater appreciation for material values. After getting his ponytail clipped by a hairstylist and investing in a three-piece suit, Jeff had gone to work for an accounting firm in Boston. Their daughter Anne had stopped scrambling over fences at army depots after her first child was born and now conducted her work for world peace from the kitchen table of her Colonial-style house in Virginia.

Marcie, their late child, had come along when Laura was thirty-eight. Once they had recovered from the shock, Marcie had been a special joy.

As had become their custom, the Cunninghams had driven up from North Carolina to spend Easter weekend with Anne, her husband, and their only grandchildren. After a cookout dinner, the children wanted to color Easter eggs, and Laura followed them good-naturedly into the bright, modern kitchen.

Laura tried to steady her four-year-old grandson's hand as he dropped the hard-boiled egg into a bowl of blue dye. She dabbed up the splashes with a paper towel as Mark proudly set his blue Easter egg beside the row of colored eggs drying on the kitchen counter.

David came in from the backyard and watched them, puffing on his old pipe.

"Who wants to hear the story of how the rabbits and bears celebrate Easter?"

"I do, Grandpa," Mark shouted happily.

"I do," six-year-old Pam echoed quietly.

As she wiped up the shiny kitchen counters, Laura listened contentedly to David's animated voice telling the Easter tale. He had always been the outgoing one. When they were younger, dating in college and early in their marriage, she had sometimes felt a little jealous of David's gregarious personality. He seemed to be the one who attracted friends.

As the years had passed, their personalities had seemed to fuse. Laura had been keenly aware of the oneness since David's heart attack the year before. She had been so grateful for David's quick recovery, so grateful when the doctor had told them the mild attack was nothing to worry about.

"Bedtime," the children's mother announced, coming into the kitchen. "You have to get to bed or the Easter bunny can't come."

Laura sighed. She was tired, weary from the long drive that

day and the constant demands of the children clamoring for attention.

"Go on up," David told her. "I'll be up as soon as I watch the eleven o'clock news."

Laura was half-asleep when David climbed into the bed beside her. She rolled over and cuddled up to him in their familiar position. Sometime later, Laura woke up suddenly and felt the empty bed beside her.

"David," she called quietly, trying not to awaken anyone. "Are you all right?"

David's muffled voice from the bathroom reassured her. Sighing, Laura pulled the sheet up around her chin and drifted off to sleep.

The next thing she knew, the sun was streaming in through the window and the pale yellow room seemed almost dazzling. Laura blinked sleepily and tried to focus on the clock on the bedside table. It was seven-thirty and the children would soon be descending upon them, expecting David to take charge of the great egg hunt.

"David," she whispered. She touched David's arm, instantly aware that something was wrong. Even through the cloth of his pajamas, his skin felt icy cold. His body was unnaturally still. She placed her hand on his chest, his face, his mouth.

Laura's heart pounded. Every nerve in her body seemed to surface. She tried to call out, but no sound came.

As she struggled to get out of bed, Laura saw the small brown bottle turned over on the bedside table and the nitroglycerin pills scattered like confetti on the plush yellow carpet.

"Oh, God," she choked. "Help me."

At that moment, Laura Cunningham was going through the most traumatic experience she would ever have to face—the sudden death of her mate.

Captured in freeze frame at that moment, her body would have shown all the symptoms of acute stress—pounding heart, sweating palms, restricted breathing.

Sara Johnston would have described the same symptoms when her husband made his lethal announcement over chilled martinis.

Richard Morrison experienced it when he stood over his young wife and realized she was dead.

So did Carol Dwyer when she unsuspectingly opened the door to a suite at the Drake Hotel.

The symptoms are a normal part of the body's protection system.

Less natural but equally normal are the social responses that forced each of them to cover up their pain and shock.

"They praised me for taking it so well," Sara said.

Richard provided a glimpse of machismo. "A man's supposed to be strong," he said.

2: REACTIONS TO SHOCK

A relative who seems happily married announces that he and his wife are getting a divorce. A business associate's wife dies of cancer. The husband of a close friend is killed in an accident.

"This will pass," we tell them, trying to strengthen them with our sympathy.

For the most part, the widowed and divorced convince us that "this" not only passes, but that the passing is brief. The divorced relative shows up at the next family reunion with the kids and a covered dish to pass. The widowed business associate talks about swinging an important business deal over lunch. The close friend assures us she's "really doing fine" and "everything is going well."

In other words, the widowed and divorced often appear to be resuming their lives pretty much as usual. They get up in the morning and go to work. They shop for groceries and drop off the cleaning. They carry on. And we observe, "It must be difficult, but that's life. People deal with it."

Behind such appearances of normality, however, most of

these people are concealing deep feelings of apprehension and fear, sometimes followed by guilt and rage.

Sara's fear that her anxiety attacks, often accompanied by sharp pains in her head, were symptoms of a complete mental breakdown or a serious physical problem is fairly common.

"I've had clients who were convinced they had a brain tumor because of the headaches," marriage therapist Susan Horwitz told us. "I encourage them to check with their doctor, but usually they find there isn't anything physically wrong with them."

A widow recalled an incident that occurred only a few days after her husband died. She was standing at the kitchen sink, and glancing through the kitchen window, she saw her husband lying on the porch glider, where he had often taken naps.

"I can't tell you how relieved I felt," the woman said. "The wake and the funeral suddenly seemed a nightmare, and I was so grateful it was over, so grateful everything was back to normal. Then I realized I had been looking at a bunched-up blanket and pillow. My husband was dead."

Like Sara, the woman feared for her sanity.

Such reactions, both physical and mental, are among the common symptoms of separation anxiety, according to sociologist Robert S. Weiss. Although "the leaver" in a marital separation may go through some of these feelings of loss, "the left" is likely to suffer the more extreme symptoms. It's important to note that in divorce situations the leaver may experience such feelings of loss over a period of up to a year or more while making the decision to leave; thus they are less intense at the end.

Weiss estimates that the recovery from a marital separation takes from two to four years, with the average closer to four. Yet the majority of those we interviewed said their families and friends started urging them to get out and meet new people within a short time, often within weeks.

The widowed and divorced do need time, but contrary to the popular belief, time alone does not "heal all wounds." Time may, indeed, dull the pain and enable the person to go on with their lives with reasonable satisfaction, but it's now generally accepted that one must go through what amounts to a mourning process before recovery and growth can take place.

Ann S. Kliman refers to the "work of mourning." As she writes, "It is indeed work—painful, hard, exhausting and often seemingly endless." The mourning process begins with allowing oneself to feel the grief. It entails recalling the countless memories and interactions with the person who is gone.

How is this accomplished, and when can this "working through" process begin? The belief that the bereaved go through five fairly predictable stages in coping with their grief is now generally accepted in the mental health field. Elisabeth Kübler-Ross first proposed the five stages of grief in her work with terminally ill patients, but the concept has been applied to any life situation involving a significant loss.

The normal, human reaction to a tragic event, divorce as well as the death of a spouse, is disbelief. This awful thing can't be happening. Why me? Such statements characterize the denial stage.

Within a fairly short time, most people recognize the tragic event has, indeed, taken place, and they're angry. The anger may be directed toward the spouse who left them, the doctor who failed to save their loved one, or, quite often, at God for permitting such an injustice.

A period of bargaining usually follows. If she only comes back, I'll be more considerate. God, give us another chance and I'll be a better person.

When all such wishful thinking fails, the person often falls into depression. The situation seems hopeless. Life is hardly worth living. This depression stage is the most recognizable and usually the most erratic of all.

A normal, healthy person can traverse the valleys of depression and arrive at the final stage of acceptance. But as we will see, the stages of grief are seldom clearly defined, and passage through them is never easy.

A CLASSIC CASE

For weeks after David Cunningham died suddenly of a heart attack, Laura rarely got out of bed.

"I couldn't believe that everything had been taken from me," she said. "Why me?"

Laura recalled the confusion after she called out for help that sunny Easter morning at her daughter's home—the sound of urgent, subdued voices in the hallway, the questioning voices of the grandchildren, the shrill sound of the ambulance siren.

Laura refused to leave the bedroom, and Anne stayed with her. They watched as the two ambulance attendants worked over David's lifeless body.

"Please, God, please."

One of the men shook his head. Without a word, they started to pack up their gear.

Later, in her daughter's shiny kitchen, still echoing with David's whimsical Easter tales, Laura tried to answer the doctor's questions. Her head throbbed; it was going to explode any minute. Her only thought was to get back home, to take David home. Perhaps in their own home, she could get her bearings and some sense of reality.

Anne was on the telephone with a local funeral director, trying to make arrangements for an ambulance to transport David's body back to North Carolina. Anne offered to drive Laura, accompanying the ambulance. Her husband could take care of making necessary telephone calls and drive down with the children on the following day.

The ambulance arrived in the late afternoon, and the driver handed Laura a release form to sign.

"The remains of David Cunningham," she read aloud from the printed form. She looked numbly at the man. "The remains?"

I interviewed Laura a year later at her home in an old section of the city. Going up the front walk, I noticed the grass needed cutting and the weeds were overtaking the flower gardens. Despite the obvious neglect, the white, two-story house had a comfortable feeling about it.

Laura greeted me warmly. Dressed in a faded blue denim skirt and striped cotton shirt, Laura had put on weight, and she wore no makeup. She had the potential of good looks—a warm, ready smile and wide, expressive blue eyes.

"At first, I couldn't believe that everything could be taken away from me," she said. "It just wasn't fair."

Laura had shown remarkable composure in making the funeral arrangements and deciding on the simple service she thought David would have wanted. Anne and Jeff had been by her side constantly, supporting her and helping with decisions. Fourteen-year-old Marcie had been summoned home from an Easter vacation with friends in Florida. Relatives had arrived from all over the country. Friends had brought casseroles, offering quiet words of sympathy.

"I felt lucky to have so much support," Laura said.

Then, having barely made a dent in all the casseroles, the crowd had departed. Laura had crawled into bed and stayed there for three days.

"I didn't want to live," Laura said. "I didn't think I had the strength to go on."

She cried. She slept fitfully. She stared into the darkness for hours, going over all that had happened the night David died. Something had awakened her that night. She had called out to David and heard his muffled reply. If she had gotten out of bed and called the doctor, perhaps something could have been done to save his life. Her negligence had possibly caused his death. Laura shook her head helplessly when

Marcie asked timidly if she wanted to get up or to eat something.

Gradually, Laura had felt the adrenaline pumping through her body. She was angry that David had been taken so suddenly, angry that she had been left with unanswered questions.

"First I was angry with God for taking David away from me," Laura said. "We had always been active in the church and we had tried to raise our children with strong religious values. I'd not only lost David, I had lost my faith in God for letting this happen."

Laura had vented her anger on everyone around her.

"I was angry with my friends for telling me I'd get over it because I thought I'd never get over it. I even became angry with David for leaving me."

For almost a year, Marcie was forced to take over the housework and the cooking. For the most part, she heated up frozen dinners, did the laundry only when she ran out of clothes, and cleaned the house when the dust started bothering her. Never more than an average student, her grades plummeted when she went back to high school that fall.

"It was hard on Marcie," Laura admitted. "She had not only lost her dad, in a way she lost me."

As she talked, Laura smoothed the denim skirt over her knees. The only jewelry she wore was her well-worn gold wedding band on the third finger of her left hand.

"I suppose I still think of myself as David's wife," Laura said, her eyes following my glance. "I think I'm gradually accepting his death. I don't know who I am without him."

"Who is Laura?" An interesting person, we would discover as she searched for her own answer.

"All things work together unto good," wrote the Apostle Paul, and indeed we would love to believe everything happens for the best.

Laura would certainly have rejected such a claim as she struggled through those early stages of grief.

The passage through the grief of separation is difficult, often ego shattering, sometimes life threatening.

"But the grief-laden do move on," Dennis Boike says, "though not as easily as Kübler-Ross's model might suggest."

One rarely passes through the grief stages in a straight, well-defined line. More common there is a maddening vacillation—two steps forward, one step back.

The grief stages are visited at least three times during the months following marital disruption.

The first run-through occurs as the person attempts to deal with the rush of feelings immediately following the event. As these emotions settle into the tenuous peace of first-level acceptance, the process rolls on to the short-term implications. What will the holidays be like alone? I'll be too broke to take the kids on vacation. That jerk is not going to spend *our* tax rebate on that round-heeled tramp. The stages take a little longer this round.

Next, the long-term consequences are faced. He won't be here to walk down the aisle and give our daughter away at her wedding. I'm going to grow old alone.

The final stage of grief is acceptance. For those who are dying, a passive acceptance may be appropriate. A man described his dying wife's attitude during her final days as "almost a willingness." He sensed she was at peace.

For the widowed and divorced, who must prepare themselves to go on living, the final stage of grief must be active acceptance followed by growth.

"Acceptance of what *is*," Dr. Boike emphasizes. "This is the first step in all anonymous groups, such as Alcoholics Anonymous, and in the initial stages of growth, reorganization, and eventual life redirection."

If these stages can be successfully completed, perhaps Paul wasn't so idealistic after all.

GRIEF DENIED

Unlike Laura, who went through fairly predictable stages of grief, Judy Carpenter appeared cool and aloof after she and her husband, a college professor, agreed to end their marriage after fifteen years together.

"I thought we could work it out until I found out he was cheating on me," Judy said, arching an eyebrow. "He actually took one of his graduate students to Palm Springs and charged the hotel and meals on our Visa. Can you believe that?"

Judy and their fourteen-year-old daughter, Kristen, were still living in a rented duplex house near the college campus in Boulder, Colorado, where Judy's husband, Stephen, was an associate professor of American literature.

The living room was furnished simply in modern oak pieces, with colorful prints of Impressionist painters on the walls and a bowl of fresh flowers on the coffee table.

A tall, slender woman with long, naturally curly hair, Judy wore a brightly patterned Chinese-style jacket and black silk slacks. She had a delicate look about her and appeared more youthful than her thirty-five years.

"We'll stay here until Kristen finishes the school year and gets her braces off," Judy was saying. "Steve had applied for a visiting professorship in Santa Barbara, and it couldn't have come through at a better time."

Although Judy worked in the library to supplement their income, she frankly admitted she had no interest in a career. She liked being a faculty wife, enjoying the cultural activities at the college and the informal parties she gave for their friends. She welcomed students to their home, finding their ideas and enthusiasm stimulating.

Although Stephen's roving eye, his inordinate interest in his pretty female students, had long been well known around the campus, Judy had looked the other way for years.

Her sister-in-law, Nancy Harmon, had told us, "Frankly, we were surprised she stayed with him as long as she did."

Nancy had suggested Judy as a possible interview because she thought Judy's reactive behavior quite unusual. At first the Harmons had been pleased that Judy was finally getting out of a bad marriage. She appeared to be adjusting well. But the first hint of a problem came when Judy failed to show up at their house for a Christmas party. Judy had told them she would get an early start on the thirty-mile drive to their house in case the roads were slippery.

When Judy hadn't arrived by nine o'clock, Nancy's husband, Bill, slipped away from the guests and called his sister's home from the kitchen telephone.

"Kristen said Judy had left early, so we were sure she had been in an accident," Nancy said. "But Bill checked with the state patrol and no accidents had been reported in the area."

The telephone rang about midnight and Bill slipped away to the kitchen to answer it. A man identified himself as the bartender at a small bar about a mile away. He suggested Bill come after his sister.

Judy was barely coherent, and her bright green silk dress had been ripped from the neckline almost to her waist. When he first saw her, Bill thought she had been assaulted. The story he finally managed to piece together from Judy and the bartender, who was reluctant to get involved, was that Judy had come into the bar early in the evening. After having a couple of drinks alone at the bar, she had struck up a conversation with a man and they had taken a table.

The bartender's story from that point was somewhat vague. He assumed Judy and the man had left together sometime during the evening. He had been busy and hadn't noticed them again until they returned to the bar shortly before midnight. Judy had ordered a drink, and the bartender had hesitated because she appeared to be drunk. Judy had created a scene and demanded another drink.

"She isn't that kind of person," Nancy said. "She's always been, well, almost prudish."

The Christmas party was breaking up when Bill and Judy got back to the house. The Harmons put Judy to bed in the guest room and Bill called his sister's house.

Kristen answered and, obviously half-asleep, assured Bill she would be all right until morning. After a long pause, Kristen added, "I'm glad Mom's okay."

The Harmons tried to talk to Judy the next morning, but she was uncommunicative and insisted she had to get home immediately.

The drinking binges continued. Every month or so, the telephone would ring in the middle of the night, and it would be Judy or some friend of Judy's calling on Bill for help.

Between these drinking bouts, Judy appeared stoic and composed. She went to work every day at the library and continued to be as friendly and helpful as ever to the students who came in for research material.

Judy spent most of her evenings with Kristen, showing an interest in her daughter's schoolwork and her growing involvement with boys. Occasionally they went to a movie. Judy rarely went out, but one time a close friend talked her into attending a spring faculty party.

Judy's associates at the college didn't pick up a clue about her drinking or the double life she had taken up in dimly lit bars and strange beds.

"Sometimes I feel like a tramp," Judy once confided to her sister-in-law during a rare confidential talk. "I keep promising myself I'll stay out of bars. Then I start feeling depressed and convince myself I need to get out and get my mind off my problems."

Compulsive behavior is commonplace during the early stages of grief. The most obvious examples are compulsive drinking or drug use, but compulsive eating, working, talking, or sexual activity are equally common.

"One of the first things we see after a marital separation is a lot of sport screwing," Dr. Boike says. "Men feel alone, women think they aren't sexy. Both have to prove themselves."

Compulsive behavior can serve a good purpose. The man or woman who becomes temporarily obsessed by work, a hobby, or a worthy cause can buy the time needed to absorb the blow of a broken relationship. In the case of divorce, he or she may need the respite to start bolstering a battered self-esteem preparatory to addressing the real issues involved in starting life over as a single person.

If the compulsive behaviors continue for more than a few months, however, concern is justified.

Like many others, Judy failed to see the red flag. Drug and alcohol abuse are a recurring theme among the divorced and widowed.

"I read somewhere that a couple of drinks before dinner is a healthy way to relax," one man said. "There was just one problem. After those two drinks, I made the decision to have the third and fourth drink with impaired judgment. Somewhere along the line, I'd forget dinner."

A divorced man said he was so lonely he started going to bars every night. Feeling ill at ease, he'd have a few drinks.

"It wasn't long before I was getting drunk every night," he said. "Then I started smoking pot or hash, and the combination was lethal—for me, at least." He gave up drinking after several months. Just the thought had become nauseating. As he put it: "I got tired of waking up in the morning with my head in the toilet, thinking I was going to die."

A widow in her late fifties said she keeps busy during the day with her garden club and church activities. She started drinking in the evening when she became lonely and anxious.

"You've really got to watch it," she said. "You have a glass of wine to relax, a few glasses later you start feeling depressed and sorry for yourself. They say you shouldn't drink alone, but what am I going to do, invite the mailman in?"

THIS ISN'T HAPPENING

A brief period of disbelief is a normal reaction to any shock, but prolonged denial can be dangerous.

Despite the evidence, Frank Gardener couldn't accept the fact that his wife, Jill, was actually going ahead with her plans to get a divorce.

"I'd call her up almost every day for weeks after she left," Frank said. "I'd see something around the house that belonged to her and call her up to see if she wanted it. She was always polite and I suppose I kept believing she'd come back when she came to her senses. The day they delivered the divorce papers I almost went bananas."

Jill couldn't have been more specific, or for that matter more blatantly cruel, when she chose a particular day to take the children and go home to her parents.

The Gardeners had been married for almost nine years when Jill told him she was in love with another man, one of the couple's best friends, and wanted a divorce.

"We'd had arguments, but I didn't think we had a serious problem," Frank said. "Most of the arguments were over my job and how much time I was away from home."

As an external auditor for a manufacturing company, Frank traveled regularly between the company's branches. His trips ranged from a few days to several weeks.

Jill complained that she had raised their two children, ages five and eight, with almost no help from Frank. He was never there when a child came down with the measles or fell out of a tree and had to be taken to the hospital emergency room. He never seemed to be around for the Christmas pageants, the dance recitals, or the birthday parties.

"I knew she hated my absences, and it was no picnic for me," Frank said. "But I like my job and it paid the bills."

When I met Frank for the first time, Jill had already filed for divorce. She and the children were staying with her parents temporarily, and Frank was still living in their two-bedroom tract house.

A tall, slim man with jet-black hair, Frank apologized for the messy condition of the house, making no mention of his own unkempt appearance. The black stubble on his unshaven face exaggerated the natural pallor of his skin. His baggy gray running suit obviously hadn't been washed recently.

"We moved here when we were first married, thinking it would be just a starter house," Frank was saying as he cleared off the kitchen table and piled more dirty dishes into an already filled sink. "Somehow we could never get enough money saved for a down payment on a better place."

But, he added after filling the coffeepot and setting out clean cups, "I thought we were pretty happy here."

Frank described an apparently idealized picture of a close-knit neighborhood, bonded by the common problems of raising families and keeping up with constantly rising expenses. The neighbors helped each other, entertained each other, and, he admitted, often gossiped about each other.

"Kathy and Mike Fisher were our best friends," Frank said. "Being away so much, I was glad they were always there to help Jill out if any emergency came up."

The two couples had spent a lot of time together. Jill and Kathy went back and forth to each other's houses for coffee, shared car pools, and exchanged baby-sitting. When Frank was away, Jill thought nothing of calling Mike to fix a broken disposal or show her how the circuit breakers worked.

When Frank was in town, the two couples often played cards on Saturday nights, shared a pizza, or went to a nearby tavern to dance and listen to country music.

Frank was puzzled when Kathy called him at the office one Monday morning and asked him to meet her downtown for lunch. Had she misinterpreted his affectionate squeeze when he had asked her to dance on Saturday night? Admittedly, he'd had a few too many beers.

"What's up?" he asked Kathy warily.

Kathy refused to explain over the phone. But before she hung up, she pleaded, "Please don't mention this to Jill."

Frank was uncomfortable, on guard, when he arrived at the coffee shop near his office and found Kathy waiting. She was obviously agitated.

"I think my husband and your wife are having an affair," she said as soon as he was seated opposite her in the red plastic booth.

This was the last thing Frank had expected to hear. He shook his head in disbelief.

"I've suspected for some time," Kathy said, her voice trembling. "It wasn't anything I could really put my finger on until one night last week. You were out of town and Mike had gone down to help Jill move some furniture. He had a phone call from his boss, and I decided I'd better run down to get him. I started to knock, but I saw them through the window. They were kissing."

Frank tried to think of a logical explanation. "We're good friends," he said. "Maybe it was just a friendly kiss."

Kathy watched him quietly. She was calmer now.

"I don't think so," she said.

Surely there was a logical explanation, Frank told himself that afternoon. He planned to ask Jill as soon as he got home. But for some reason, he kept putting it off until they were in their bedroom getting ready for bed. Even then it was awkward. He could hardly bring himself to say the words.

"Is there something going on between you and Mike?"

Jill carefully put her hairbrush on the dressing table. When she finally looked at him, her eyes were filled with tears. She sat down, almost collapsed, on the bed, and started crying. Between sobs, she blurted out the story of how she and Mike had tried to deny they were in love, how much she had hated the subterfuge.

"I've wanted to tell you," she said finally. "I want a divorce."

Frank shook his head in disbelief. She would come to her senses, he told himself as he packed for a business trip the following morning. Jill set out the cereal and called the children as if nothing had happened.

Weeks passed. Frank's work schedule was heavy at this year-end time, and he was away more than ever. When he was home, Jill seemed absorbed in her Christmas lists.

"The kids want new bikes," she told Frank one evening. "Do you think we can afford it?"

Frank waited for the other shoe to drop.

The holiday season had been a difficult time emotionally for Frank ever since his mother died on December 21 when he was fifteen years old. Five years later, on December 21, he had crashed his car into a bridge culvert and spent the holidays in the hospital. December 21 had taken on an ominous meaning ever since, and every year he approached it with apprehension. He was always relieved when the holidays were over.

"Jill knew that," Frank said. "And that year, when I got home from work on December 21, she was gone. I was a basket case."

Feeling anxious and confused, Frank called Jill almost every day until her father threatened to have him arrested for harassment.

"I couldn't seem to accept the fact that she wanted to leave me," Frank said with a helpless gesture. "For my best friend, at that."

A kind, gentle person himself, Frank couldn't accept the

obvious fact that Jill had not only left, but had tried to hurt him in the process.

"Frank needs to get in touch with reality," Dr. Boike concludes. "He seems to have no conception that his wife is a real person with feelings. All the way up until the time Jill left, he didn't do a thing. He refused to leave the safety of his fictional Fantasy Island, where everything could be as his heart desired. What he wanted was Jill. It's nice to come home to a cooked meal and clean laundry."

For Frank, and for many others who remain stuck in the early stages of grief, there are some distinct payoffs to denial.

First of all, there is no need to worry about the future turning out all wrong: it's guaranteed. Frank even had a ready date for it, and Jill was prepared to accommodate him, perhaps as a way of finally waking him up.

Second, the person who is stuck can preserve the illusion of being the "aggrieved partner" and point the finger at the "real culprit." It may seem like a small reward for committing psychological suicide, but for some people it represents self-vindication and self-righteousness.

Just as some people get stuck in denial, others are trapped by their anger. Expressing anger in a healthy, nondestructive way is difficult. Women who have been brought up to be passive and agreeable may have unconsciously trained themselves to suppress anger. Moreover, men as well as women may associate anger with being out of control, often regarded as a sign of weakness in our culture. In such instances, suppressed anger can, and often does, explode into rage and sometimes violence. Lethal threats against an ex-spouse or third party are all too common, and the daily newspaper reports prove there are those who carry out their threats, resorting to weapons and force as the handiest solution to the frustrations of a love triangle.

I CAN'T GO ON

Depression is usually the most erratic and confusing condition for the bereaved to pass through.

Laura Cunningham had considered herself a fairly happy person until her husband, David, died suddenly of a heart attack. Then depression descended over her like a heavy black veil.

"I didn't want to live," Laura said. "I didn't think I had the strength to go on."

Laura's depression was, at times, severe and debilitating, and apparently her feelings are quite typical. An estimated 95 percent of women consider suicide at some point during the mourning process.

Suicide occurred to her, Laura admitted. But, she explained, "It wasn't so much that I wanted to die. I just didn't want to go on living. You simply get careless. Like you don't bother to look both ways before you cross the street."

Depression is commonly characterized by feelings of loss, lack of hope for the future, and a sense of helplessness.

Death is socially acceptable in the widowed because their loss is obvious: death occurs. Divorce is another matter. We assume the divorce is what at least one spouse wanted. There is a certain degree of choice.

Yet the loss is just as real. Often one partner has no choice. This person has not only lost a loved one, he or she has been rejected. They've been told by their partner's actions, if not words, "You are no longer needed. You are no longer essential to my happiness."

If one partner asks for the divorce, they may initially feel relieved or even euphoric, but eventually the loss must be faced.

"I've found the relief usually lasts about three to six weeks," Dr. Boike says. "During this period, the person will talk about the good decision they've made. Then the reality comes in and they have to face the loss."

The depression that follows the breakup of an unhappy marriage is even harder to understand.

"People get confused," says marriage therapist Susan Horwitz. "A client will say, 'Why am I grieving? He was a real bastard.' Often they're grieving for what might have been."

When an unhappy marriage breaks up, the mixed feelings that follow may be further complicated by guilt. The person who is prone to critical self-examination will probably ask, "Could I have saved the marriage if I had tried harder?" The person with a predisposition for taking blame will have a field day when the symptoms of grief set in. Just look at the unhappiness they've brought upon themselves and others!

The severe depression that follows the initial shock is usually followed by recurring attacks of a milder form. A birthday, an anniversary, a holiday, even the first days of spring when everyone else appears to be happy can bring on a bout of depression.

"That first year of holidays can really knock you out," said a woman who helped set up a support group in her church. "We try to make sure none of our members spend their first holidays alone."

Depression is a normal, essential step in working through the process of mourning. The grief must be felt, no matter how understanding or sophisticated the person may be.

Severe or prolonged depression is not normal, however. The person who consistently expresses absolute hopelessness may be on the brink of suicide.

CHILDREN MUST GRIEVE, TOO

Children often see the loss of a parent by death or divorce as the loss of both parents. One parent is physically gone, the other is psychologically removed.

Laura looked back on the experience of her daughter, Marcie, and summed it up well.

"She not only lost her dad, in a way she lost me."

At fourteen and going through a time of transition herself, Marcie lost the support of two loving parents. She had no outlet for the grief she was feeling and, in fact, had to take over her mother's responsibilities around the house. No wonder she was anxious and upset. No wonder her school grades dropped.

Children need to express grief at their own level, and this may be especially difficult for young children.

Author and family therapist Ruth Jean Loewinsohn tells the poignant story of a four-year-old child who had gone to her father's funeral and visited his grave. Unable to understand the finality of death, the child later started sobbing and pounding on her mother's stomach.

"It's your fault Daddy died," the child cried. "You didn't water Daddy. If you had watered his grave, he would have grown again like the plants do."

Loewinsohn used this illustration in her *Survival Handbook for Widows* to show how important it is to explain the death of a parent to preschool children in terms they can understand. Since children under six see the world in concrete terms, Loewinsohn suggests that religious explanations of death may be confusing. A child who is told that "God decided He wanted your mother to be with Him," the way Peggy Morrison's death was explained to her children by her mother, may take the statement literally. The child may start wondering, "What if He decides He wants me?" or, "What if He wants Daddy?"

Young children go through a period of magical thinking, usually from about age five to ten, when they believe they can control what happens around them. Remember "Step on a crack and break your mother's back"? Children who think magically may be unable to discriminate between fantasy and reality and believe they're responsible for their parent's death.

They may feel anxious and insecure about what is going to happen to them.

In her crisis intervention work with families, Ann Kliman found that young children express their grief in a variety of ways appropriate for their age. A four-year-old boy became anxious after his sister died of crib death. Thinking he had somehow caused his sister's death, he started wetting the bed, became apprehensive about going to bed, and cried over nothing. A twelve-year-old thought he was crazy because he had hallucinations in which his dead father appeared to be standing in the doorway of his bedroom.

These children needed to understand that their reactions were normal and appropriate.

"Young children mourn differently from adults, but they do mourn, and they can do most of the work of mourning with the help of important adults around them," Kliman writes.

A separation or divorce may be difficult for children to accept if the parents appeared to be getting along.

"My teenage son was angry with me for a whole year after the divorce," one mother said. "He kept telling me what a terrible thing I'd done to him."

Children often try to get their parents back together. Young children, still in the stage of magical thinking, may promise to behave better if the absent parent will just come home.

A five-year-old girl watched her three-year-old sister have a temper tantrum a few weeks after their mother moved out of the house.

"Dad, she just hasn't got it yet," the five-year-old explained to their father.

Sometimes children "get it" even before the adults. If there has been an increase in arguments and tension in the home, the announcement of a separation or divorce usually comes as no surprise to the children. If one parent has been abusive or alcoholic, their reaction to the breakup may initially be relief.

As Dr. Boike puts it, "Parents forget it's the kids' event, too."

As dramatic and frightening as it may be, the widowed and divorced must fully experience the normal, human responses to the loss of an intimate relationship. The stages of grief—denial, anger, bargaining, depression—lead to the final stage of acceptance and regrowth.

If Laura had fully understood the mourning process, perhaps she would not have fallen into mindless apathy and stayed that way so long. If Judy had accepted her feelings as normal, perhaps she would not have chosen such self-destructive behavior. And if Frank had known the rewards to be gained, maybe he could have faced the reality of his situation.

In their own ways, each of them chose to remain stuck and to accept the small payoffs that "stuckness" brings. Laura could say, "Poor me." Judy could say, "Who cares?" And Frank could point a finger at the villains who did him in.

Of course the death of a spouse, as natural as it may be, isn't just another life event, and a divorce isn't just a second chance to swing back into the singles scene. The expectations of others may be partly to blame for the victims' denial.

For everyone involved, death and divorce are major life crises—painful, traumatic, even life threatening. They must therefore be accepted and dealt with.

We followed their stories—Sara, Richard, Carol, Laura, Judy, Frank—as they adjusted to the drastic changes in their lives. For some, overcoming adversity led to a happier, more satisfying life. For others, recovery was never quite complete.

3: THE LEGAL ASPECTS

The terms of a divorce settlement can have a major impact on the life of a person long after the divorce is final, but unfortunately many people agree to those terms while still suffering from shock or while under extreme duress.

"I finally got to a point when I would have signed almost anything to get it over with," Sara Johnston reflected. "I tried to be rational and think about my future, but the fact is, my sanity was at stake. At least I thought so at the time."

Frank Gardener, unable to fully accept the fact that his wife was leaving him, turned everything over to a lawyer who was not familiar with matrimonial laws. Frank hired the lawyer only because he knew the man personally. Later he blamed the lawyer for costing him extra money and for cutting him off from his two young children.

"I assumed a lawyer is a lawyer and should be qualified to handle any type of case. When you hire a professional, you assume they know their business."

Frank's passive attitude, leaving everything up to his lawyer, is fairly typical. At the other extreme is the vindictive spouse pushing for everything he or she can get. Some clients alternate between the two, being apathetic one day and vengeful the next. Such mood swings are often triggered by some real or imagined fear of what the spouse may be up to, and they can make special demands on the lawyer.

"I get a lot of nervous phone calls in the evening," says Richard Williams, who has specialized in divorce cases since he joined an eleven-member upstate New York law firm eight years ago. "I suppose I encourage that by taking a personal interest in my cases, but I think that's important. You're dealing with a lot of personal matters in a divorce case."

Williams says some divorce lawyers won't take telephone calls at home, but he notes, "I can't do that. I think you can be professional without being aloof."

Keeping the lawyer-client relationship on a professional basis can be a problem when the lawyer takes a personal interest. The client begins to gravitate toward you as a person. Williams's rules for conduct include having all meetings with clients in his office and turning down invitations to "celebrate" over a drink or dinner.

Although lawyers appear reluctant to talk about it, as in any care-giving profession, some lawyers take advantage of their clients' vulnerable emotional state. As we shall see, Judy Carpenter's lawyer stepped over the line between professional and personal involvement into an intimate relationship.

A divorced woman in her late fifties admitted to having dated her lawyer during her divorce from a wealthy man several years ago. She still sees nothing wrong with it and, in fact, recalls welcoming the opportunity to talk about personal matters over drinks or an occasional dinner.

A professional woman in her thirties expressed another viewpoint.

"I was paying my lawyer ninety dollars an hour," she said. "At those prices, I resented the time he spent advising me on personal matters like selling my house and what to do about the children's schooling. I wanted legal advice because that's what I was paying him for."

I THINK I NEED A LAWYER

Sara Johnston stepped off the ornate vintage elevator into the marble, high-ceilinged hallway and looked around her at the series of closed paneled doors. Each had names in black Gothic lettering engraved on frosted glass.

Sara recalled entering this downtown lawyers' building only twice before. She and Jim had come here to sign papers at their house closing and again to revise their wills. There was something stiff and forbidding about this legal bastion, and Sara was sorry she had come alone.

"My husband has left me," Sara said nervously after the distinguished, gray-haired man had introduced himself and asked her to be seated in a green leather chair. "I think I need a lawyer."

Sara had followed the advice of a good friend and made an appointment with an attorney who specialized in matrimonial law. Initially she had agreed to go along with Jim's suggestion that they let their family lawyer handle their divorce. Jim had assured her he wanted to be fair about dividing up their joint property. He wanted to part amicably.

But when Sara heard that Jim had sold his dental equipment and applied for a loan to open a marina and boatyard, she began to have misgivings. Clearly, Jim was moving ahead with his plans and would no doubt continue to live the affluent life they had become accustomed to. Sara was concerned about how she was going to manage financially. Going directly from college into the marriage, she had never supported herself independently of her husband, and she wasn't sure she could do it now.

"Have you thought about what you might want in a settlement?"

The lawyer was speaking and Sara tried to concentrate. Why did this meeting feel so much like a betrayal of Jim? After all, Jim had betrayed her.

"Not really," Sara said, shaking her head helplessly. "My husband says he wants to be fair, but he doesn't really seem concerned about what happens to me. He's acting just in his own interests."

Tactfully turning the conversation around, the attorney questioned Sara about her life-style, personal assets, her work experience, and her opportunities for full-time employment. He told her his fee was $150 an hour, higher than the local average, but he felt sure he could get a satisfactory settlement for her.

"He was answering all the questions I should have asked," Sara said later. "I look back on that period and realize how helpless and vulnerable I was during that time."

At the lawyer's request, Sara collected certain documents, including birth certificates, their marriage license, deeds to property she and Jim owned jointly, and copies of their income tax records for the past two years. She made copies of these documents for her lawyer to use until the originals were needed in court.

The lawyer asked Sara to compile a budget of their joint expenses for the past year and to estimate her current personal expenses as accurately as possible.

After going over these figures, Sara's lawyer told her a simple division of joint property wouldn't be fair to her. She should be entitled to a continuation of health insurance and a share of the retirement account Jim had built up during the years of their marriage.

Sara had also made nonmonetary contributions to the marriage for twenty-six years, her lawyer pointed out. She had worked while Jim completed dental school, contributing to his earning power. And as a result of giving up her career to raise the children, her own earning power had decreased.

Since Jim presumably wanted the divorce, he should be willing to negotiate, the lawyer pointed out.

Sara wasn't sure what to do, but then she learned that Jim

had moved in with a woman who used to work as his dental assistant. Upset by this new development, Sara screwed up her resolve and urged her lawyer to get everything he could out of her ex-spouse. A few months later, impatient with how long the process was taking, she shifted again and told her lawyer to settle for anything he could get. She wanted to get it over with.

In retrospect, Sara believed she was too unstable during that time to make rational decisions. She gave her attorney credit for making her aware of her legal rights, collecting the essential facts in the case, and making a convincing presentation at the divorce hearing.

But it wasn't easy for her even at the end. "I had a severe anxiety attack as we were going into the judge's chambers," Sara said. "I just sat there, praying I wouldn't pass out, and my lawyer did most of the talking."

Sara's lawyer asked for half the couple's joint property, including the house, full payment of Sara's college expenses for two years of graduate work, a maintenance allowance for two years, a continuation of health coverage, and half of Jim's retirement benefits contributed during the years of their marriage.

The judge awarded the full settlement, and Jim's lawyer said his client didn't wish to contest it. If Jim had decided to contest the settlement, the case would have gone to trial.

"He didn't contest it because he knew the settlement was fair," Sara's lawyer pointed out. "In a divorce case, there aren't any winners. Everybody ends up hurting a little."

Sara's story is a good example of a competent, aggressive attorney preventing an injustice without adding to his client's problems. Sara's attorney helped her to realize she needed to protect her position. His homework in preparing a strong case made it possible to achieve a settlement without the need of a trial, which is always desirable.

Jim's new relationship, upsetting as it was to Sara, was not a factor. In most states grounds for divorce have been almost entirely separated from the issue of an appropriate financial settlement, a positive change because it cuts out the dirty laundry issues that once played a key part in divorce cases.

Sara, who would decide to get professional counseling after her divorce was final, regretted she didn't make that decision earlier. She might have benefited from counseling while she was going through the heavy emotional issues involved in the divorce.

Fortunately, Sara's attorney dealt with her mood swings and dependent behavior in a tactful, businesslike way.

NOT JUST ANY LAWYER

Frank Gardener regretted he hadn't put more thought and time into the selection of a lawyer.

"I went to my dad's lawyer because he was the only lawyer I knew," Frank said. "I met him through some real estate deals he had handled for the family and got to know him fairly well. I thought I could trust him."

The Gardeners' divorce looked like a simple case because they had so few assets to divide. After nine years of marriage, they owned a small equity in their house, a station wagon about half paid off, and various furniture they had accumulated. Frank had a pension plan at work. For the most part, they had lived from month to month, and at the time of the divorce, they had no money in savings.

Jill wanted the house and agreed to obtain a second mortgage in order to pay Frank his share of the equity. Frank took the station wagon and Jill kept the furniture.

The judge ordered monthly child support payments of $100 for each child and no alimony for Jill. Frank thought the settlement was fair. He also agreed to weekend visitation rights by prior arrangement with Jill. Having no reason to think Jill would try to keep him from seeing the children, the informal arrangement seemed ideally suited to his irregular work schedule.

Later, however, Frank decided the family's friendly lawyer, unfamiliar with issues in divorce cases, had sold him down the river.

"He didn't go into details like who would take the children as a tax deduction," Frank said. "I had to thrash these things out with Jill when they came up, and I usually lost."

Jill and Mike got married as soon as their divorces were final. Mike moved in with Jill. His former wife, Kathy, and their children still lived down the street. Jill and Kathy avoided seeing each other, and their children no longer played together.

"I was against paying Jill alimony at the time of the divorce," Frank said. "As it turned out, alimony would have been tax deductible and my responsibility would have ended when Jill remarried."

Frank also regretted that his visitation rights weren't spelled out.

"If I'm late with my support payment, Jill can always find some reason why it isn't convenient for me to see the kids that weekend. She's got this hanging over me until the kids are eighteen."

Knowing Jill might try to hassle him if the support payment was late, Frank sometimes went for weeks without attempting to see his children. This wasn't fair to him or his children, he agreed, but he felt like Jill had him over the proverbial barrel.

Actually, Frank ended up with a reasonable settlement. Less than $25 a week per child is a small amount for child support, and unlike alimony, it ends when the children "emancipate."

Unstructured visitation rights are usually preferable because they allow for a degree of flexibility for the children, which is desirable. Moreover, Frank was not limited to the convenience of his former wife: he could have petitioned the court for a fixation of visitation rights.

Frank's inexperienced lawyer failed to make clear his client's options. Custody and visitation rights are never written in stone, and lawyers should always explain in detail the possible effects of a settlement and the reasons behind recommending it.

Frank's lawyer was lax in overlooking important details, such as who would take the children as a tax deduction, and for failing to fully explain the reasoning behind the settlement. Frank added to the problem by failing to take the initiative. He should have asked his lawyer's advice on how to handle his visitation problems. The lawyer-client relationship should not end with the signing of the divorce agreement.

WHAT TO EXPECT FROM A LAWYER

The two stories illustrate some important points concerning the lawyer's role in a divorce case.

Except in rare cases of amicable preagreement, each party should be represented by a different attorney, with no personal connection to either party.

If one party doesn't want the divorce, or the couple can't agree on the custody of the children, or there is considerable property involved, their lawyers should be expected to resolve these issues through negotiation and litigation.

Sara's story illustrates a fairly recent trend toward placing value on the wife's nonmonetary contributions to the marriage. A New York State Supreme Court justice in White Plains ordered a doctor to pay his former wife $188,000 over a ten-year period. This was the calculated value of her contribution to his increased income. Appellate judges threw out the award, and at this time, the case in still in litigation.

The concept behind nonmonetary contributions is simply that marriage is a partnership and the working spouse benefits financially from that partnership. The joint bank account is divided, so why not the "joint business"? The concept is good, but valuation is extremely difficult. The trend today, at least in some states, appears to be in the direction of arbitrary fixed percentages rather than taking each case on its own merits. Under a recent New York decision, the nonworking spouse automatically receives 50 percent of the working spouse's pension benefits without regard to the real relative contributions of the spouses to the marriage partnership itself. The trend may well carry over to the valuation of business and professional income.

The two stories also illustrate the importance of hiring an attorney who either specializes in matrimonial law or who is experienced in this area. Divorce laws vary from state to state and are constantly changing. Based on his experience and knowledge of the law, Sara's attorney knew a simple division of property would not be fair in her case. On the other hand, Frank's attorney overlooked simple points and, apparently, didn't communicate well with his client. The emotional state of the client was a factor in both cases. Beyond the obvious considerations of competency and honesty, a divorce lawyer should be sensitive to the client's state of mind and assume the role of advocate when necessary.

Finding the right lawyer is similar to choosing any professional. Local bar associations or the American Association of Matrimonial Lawyers will usually provide the names of several attorneys who specialize in matrimonial law. As one attorney advises, "Talk to friends who are divorced and ask a lot of questions. Ask them how they were treated and how the lawyer presented the case in court. There's more to it than the settlement."

A competent lawyer will be glad to arrange a preliminary interview before taking a case. The client should ask how long the lawyer has been practicing in the state and what percentage of the lawyer's practice involves matrimonial cases. Will the attorney handle the case personally? Who will take over in an emergency?

Fees should be discussed up front. Most lawyers charge an hourly rate, and some require a retainer. The cost of a divorce varies so widely between states, and between cities and small communities, that an "average" figure is almost meaningless. Estimates run from $1,500 to $5,000 per case. An attorney should be willing to estimate the cost after a preliminary interview.

The attorney can also be expected to advise the client on divorce laws in that state and to give general advice on a fair distribution of property and an appropriate child custody arrangement.

Lawyers should not be expected to give personal or financial advice, especially if they are not trained in psychology or money management, although sometimes they can offer suggestions to be used as general guidelines. In the way a real estate lawyer becomes familiar with property values, an experienced divorce lawyer has probably observed certain patterns that seem to have worked over time.

Lawyers should not be expected to listen to lengthy complaints about what "the other party" is doing unless it has some bearing on the case, nor should they be expected to take unnecessary telephone calls, especially at home.

Of course, there can be exceptional situations. "Legal problems don't always arise between nine and five, Monday through Friday," attorney Richard Williams points out. "Visitation problems, for example, rarely crop up until the last minute. A call to the other party with the line 'I just spoke to my lawyer and he said if you don't abide by the court order, you will be in court by tomorrow afternoon' can be a very effective method of solving the problem. Providing this kind of support shows the lawyer isn't 'just in it for the money' but has a personal commitment to the case and to the client.

"Lawyers should be sympathetic to the emotional devastation which is caused by divorce," he adds. "I've had many, many clients who simply need to be reassured from time to time that there is a light at the end of the tunnel. It may be like a doctor saying, 'Take two aspirins and call me in the morning.' The 'aspirins' may not help, but at least the client knows the lawyer will be there tomorrow."

THE BARRACUDAS

Almost every city has certain lawyers who have built their reputations on winning divorce cases by ruthless tactics. Not always respected, these lawyers are well known by their colleagues and professionals in the marriage and divorce fields.

"When a woman asks my advice on getting a lawyer, I ask them what they want to accomplish," says marriage therapist Susan Horwitz. "Some women just want a fair settlement, but others want to go for the balls."

Elizabeth Erickson was definitely in the latter category.

"Gordon took the position that, having supported me for twenty-four years, he owed me nothing," Elizabeth said. "I wanted to strip him down to his underwear, the bastard."

Elizabeth and Gordon had grown apart, and neither seemed interested in trying to mend the gap. Elizabeth liked to play bridge and throw memorable parties. Gordon enjoyed classical music and the arts. They had accommodated each other for years without any real communication between them. Elizabeth's party guests sometimes tracked Gordon down in his den to tell him they had a good time. Since he was usually absorbed in listening to music, often they didn't bother. Elizabeth went to concerts only if they qualified as a social event. Gordon roamed the art galleries alone.

The marriage might have gone on that way if Gordon hadn't met a woman who shared his interests. The woman wasn't young—only a year younger than Elizabeth, in fact—but Gordon had caught a glimpse of what his life could be like.

When Gordon told Elizabeth he wanted a divorce, she was furious. A longshoreman would have blushed at her language. No tears. No remorse. No emotion.

Gordon had hoped they could talk. He had wanted to provide for Elizabeth's future, to help her continue the kind of life she had enjoyed and could easily continue without him. Elizabeth's reaction surprised and angered him. Normally a soft-spoken, easygoing man, Gordon saw Elizabeth for the first time, and what he saw was an indolent, unappreciative woman. He packed an overnight bag and left, pausing just long enough to inform Elizabeth that he wouldn't give her a penny.

Elizabeth was not intimidated. After a few discreet inquiries about the toughest divorce lawyer in the city, Elizabeth made an appointment with Sam Turner.

A small, wiry man with a shock of bushy white hair, Sam showed his flair for getting right to the point.

"How much is he worth? Is he shacking up?"

Gordon, who owned an advertising agency in Cleveland, was worth enough to make Sam's eyes light up. As for living with the other woman, Gordon was too prudent to move in with the new interest in his life, and Elizabeth knew it.

But that didn't daunt Sam. By the time they were prepared to go into court, Sam had "the goods" on Gordon—circumstantial evidence, including photographs, witnesses, and a slanted deposition from the other woman's landlady.

On Sam's advice, Elizabeth wore a simple but attractive

dress for her court appearance and about half the jewelry she normally wore.

After a run-through with Sam, Elizabeth quietly told the judge she had been nervous and upset since Gordon left her. She was suffering from severe headaches and a recently troubling congenital back problem that prevented her from working.

Sam called Elizabeth's doctor as a witness. The doctor testified he had been treating Elizabeth for migraine headaches and back pains.

"Yes," the doctor replied under Sam's questioning. "These could be symptoms of acute stress."

Gordon's lawyer pointed out that his client's behavior should have no bearing on the settlement. But Sam, who had taken the case on a contingency basis, was eloquent in his final summary before the judge. Even Elizabeth was impressed.

Sam had made an issue of Gordon's financial worth, including the couple's expensive home in the affluent Cleveland suburb of Shaker Heights. The judge awarded Elizabeth a substantial cash settlement and alimony.

Elizabeth had the house completely redecorated. She continued to play bridge almost every afternoon, and after a decent period of resting her bad back, she resumed her memorable parties.

Very often the only thing barracuda lawyers really sink their teeth into is the pocketbook of their clients. It's important to remember that the judge makes the decision, and judges tend to be more impressed by facts than by questionable "evidence" or emotional eloquence.

Since the Ericksons were well off financially, Elizabeth would probably have gotten a substantial settlement under any circumstances. Furthermore, Sam may have collected more than his share of the bounty. Contingency fees are questionable in matrimonial cases and not permitted in some states.

THE OVERINVOLVED LAWYER

Judy Carpenter may have appeared as cool and aloof as Elizabeth, but there was no comparison in their personalities. Elizabeth was tough; Judy was naive. In fact, for a woman of thirty-five, Judy was surprisingly innocent.

Her naiveté and fragile beauty aroused the sympathy of one of the busiest lawyers in Boulder. After hearing Judy's story in her preliminary visit, Matt Fisher agreed not only to take her case, but to reduce his usual fee.

"Matt was so strong and kind," Judy said later. "I liked the feeling of being protected."

Matt was in his mid-thirties, divorced for six years, and good-looking. He was considered "a catch" but carefully avoided any lasting relationship, never pairing with the same woman at social affairs more than once or twice. People gossiped about this woman or that but had to allow that his law practice came first. Judy, who had moved in an entirely different social circle at the college, was not aware of Matt's popularity with women.

"You need to get away and forget your problems," Matt said one evening after they had left his office and stopped for coffee. "Let's go to Denver next weekend."

The spontaneous invitation charmed Judy. "Wonderful idea," she agreed.

On Saturday they explored the city, and that evening they went to a play. Soaking in the bathtub before dressing to go out, Judy realized she felt relaxed and happy. She hadn't thought about Stephen or the divorce all day. Her problems seemed far away. She didn't want the weekend to end.

"Wonderful play," Judy said over a late dinner at a rooftop restaurant. "I've never laughed so hard."

They lingered over their coffee, enjoying the view of the skyline and the clear, starry night. Judy was almost disappointed when Matt kissed her lightly at the door of her room and wished her good night.

She sighed as she closed the door and leaned thoughtfully against it. Then she glanced at her bed and smiled.

A single red rose rested against the snowy-white pillow of her turned-down bed. A bottle of champagne in a pail of ice and two glasses were on the bedside table.

Humming softly, Judy put on her pale yellow nightgown and negligee. She dialed Matt's room.

"I seem to have champagne for two," she said.

"Isn't that odd? I'd be glad to help you out."

The affair that began that night continued, and the lovers appeared oblivious to the possible consequences.

Judy and Matt paid dearly for their romantic interludes.

Confident he could convince the court that Judy was a wronged woman, Matt emphasized Stephen's philanderings with his students. To his surprise and chagrin, Stephen's colleagues at the college refused to appear as witnesses. A graduate student who had agreed to testify that Stephen had seduced her backed out at the last minute. The publicity could ruin her chances for getting a job, she told Matt.

The judge was openly annoyed that Matt's accusations against Stephen appeared to be based entirely on gossip and hearsay.

Stephen's lawyer had not been idle. Witnesses testified that Judy and Stephen had participated regularly in college functions and appeared to have a good marriage. Judy had filed for the divorce, and her job at the library proved she was capable of supporting herself.

In a final coup, the lawyer subpoenaed a bartender whose testimony proved Judy had not been leading an exemplary life. Judy was called to the stand and questioned about where she had spent certain nights and with whom. Although Matt was never identified as one of Judy's lovers, he was openly disturbed by this new information. Judy began to see her chances for getting custody of Kristen slipping away.

"I lost everything, including my self-respect," Judy said. "By the time it was over, I felt lucky to get joint custody of my daughter."

The judge ordered the joint custody after a private conference with Kristen, who had established her loyalty to both parents. The judge turned down Judy's request for alimony and child support. Under the ruling, Stephen was responsible for Kristen's medical expenses and education costs.

The judge warned Judy she could lose her joint custody rights if she continued to drink heavily and to set a poor example of moral values.

"I thought it was the real thing with Matt," Judy said after the decision. "Love at last. He wouldn't even talk to me after the hearing. I guess he was shocked by all that came out about me, but he could have listened to my side of the story."

Judy decided her only chance for the future was to leave Boulder and start over.

Richard Williams's opinion of Judy's lawyer was succinct and unequivocal: "Matt's level of incompetence and lack of professional ethics should make him a candidate for disbarment. I can't believe Judy's story is at all representative of even the worst of my profession."

Certainly Judy's involvement with Matt wasn't typical of client-lawyer relationships described in our interviews, but if only a handful of lawyers become sexually involved with their clients, Judy's story is important.

A woman going through a divorce is often under extreme stress and can become emotionally dependent. The attorney may represent the only stable person in her life at that time.

In his book *The Inside of Divorce,* former divorce lawyer Bill Mortlock refers to "transference."

"Unhappy women, I have noticed, sometimes tend to form a transference very quickly indeed with a person who seems to offer comfort, relief or stability in a world grown suddenly frightening."

Judy was temporarily reassured by the sexual relationship with Matt, but another woman we interviewed described how devastated she felt when a lawyer made sexual advances during her first appointment with him.

"I spent the whole morning telling him a lot of personal things I had been going through with my husband," she said. "He told me I was obviously upset and I needed to relax. He suggested a hotel. I terminated his representation on the spot. The experience left me feeling so degraded, I've never mentioned it to anyone before, not even my family."

EASING THE PAIN WITH A MEDIATOR

The most common complaint against divorce lawyers, we found, was the adversary relationship they tend to encourage.

"My relationship with my ex-husband wasn't good, but my lawyer added fuel to the flame," was how one woman put it. "My ex-husband wanted some things I didn't have any use for, like a couple of paintings. I didn't care if he had them, but my lawyer didn't think we should let him get away with anything. By the time we got into court, we were fighting over the dish towels."

A trained mediator can operate as an objective third party capable, in many instances, of helping the couple put aside their irrational feelings in the interest of reaching fair, realistic decisions.

THE LEGAL ASPECTS 73

Mediation can be particularly helpful when there are children involved. The mediator is in the position to suggest that the couple put the best interests of their children above their feelings for each other.

"We were at each other's throats," said one man. "I couldn't even talk to her without getting angry. But I love my kids. I was willing to sit down with her and a mediator if it would help them."

Several states are either mandating mediation of child-related disputes or mandating provision of mediation services in the court system.

In California, the first state to require that all child custody and visitation disputes be mediated, the caseload has been drastically reduced, according to figures provided by the Academy of Mediators. Child custody disputes in the San Francisco courts dropped dramatically in one year.

Members of the academy are professionals in the legal or mental health fields with special training in mediation. Dr. John M. Haynes, the academy president, is an associate professor of social welfare at the State College of New York at Stony Brook.

Although the exact approach may vary, the mediator typically sits down with the couple to explain the mediation process and collect basic data. Each partner is asked to prepare a budget of his or her needs and expected income for the coming year. The mediator usually reviews the couple's federal income tax returns for the past two or three years. Sharing this information eliminates the unknown. With the information in front of them, the couple can see how much child support will be needed, the advantages of one or the other taking tax breaks, the cost of living, and housing needs. If expenses exceed income, the mediator can suggest ways to close the gap.

While their lawyers can provide the couple with some general financial guidance, discussing budgets in detail is not a lawyer's function.

The couple also makes a list of all their property and assets. If they can't agree on the distribution, the mediator can suggest a fair compromise.

Mediation tends to reduce the amount of bargaining room the two parties may try to create with inflated or deflated values on property. In a typical divorce, both parties might attempt to get the house appraised at a higher or lower value depending upon their interests. In mediation, the couple agrees to use the same data.

The mediator helps the couple decide which items are liquid and which are fixed. There may be an advantage to remaining partners in the retaining of some assets. They could decide to hold a bond due to mature in five years, for example, rather than paying a penalty for cashing it in before maturity.

Once they have an agreement in writing, the mediator may suggest that both parties take a copy to their respective lawyers to make it legally binding and to protect their rights.

The mediation process is still new enough to be somewhat controversial. Its proponents say that it brings the couple face to face: they can't then hide behind their attorneys to explain their actions or make unreasonable demands. Also, successful mediation can save the couple time and money.

On the other hand, skeptics make the point that couples who go into mediation are probably reasonable people who could solve their problems without the mediator, saving themselves even more time and money.

And as those on both sides of the issue agree, some couples may have differences too complex to resolve in mediation. Certain issues can only be resolved through litigation in the courts.

Furthermore, if mediation fails, the couple may have to go back to square one in the divorce process.

THE LAWYER-THERAPIST TEAM

With people becoming more and more sensitive to the emotional impact of divorce, some lawyers are teaming up with therapists to work out divorce settlements.

The lawyer and therapist may form a partnership that combines the therapist's communication skills with the lawyer's knowledge of the legal aspects in the case.

The therapist encourages the couple to talk about their fears, their goals for the future, and the kind of relationship they want to have with their children after the divorce. If the husband has been the primary breadwinner, he may be worried about the financial drain of alimony and child support. If the wife hasn't worked or has provided the secondary income, she may be worried about supporting herself, or herself and her children. Young professional couples who have relied on two incomes to pay the mortgage payments and buy the groceries may be worried about how they're going to manage on one income. Parents have concerns about what will happen to their children, particularly if the other party gets custody.

These fears are often the underlying cause for angry confrontations between couples and a general antagonism that can lead to battling out differences in court. A skilled therapist can help the couple express their feelings and alleviate some of the anger and frustration that often build up in the process of divorce.

The lawyer-therapist team is still a fairly new professional alternative, and some divorce lawyers and therapists work together on a referral basis.

"If I get a client who's crying a lot, I suggest they see a therapist I've worked with," said one attorney.

Lawyers and therapists both allow that a gap still exists between the legal and mental health professions. Joint professional conferences have been one attempt to bring them together, but despite such efforts only about 9 or 10 percent of divorcing couples seek counseling.

"We're trying to get that number up," one therapist said. "The earlier we can intervene, the more helpful we can be. Too many lawyers are setting themselves up as all-knowing. I don't give my clients legal advice. I wish lawyers wouldn't give psychological advice."

STOREFRONT LAWYERS

Legal clinics are springing up all over the country offering legal services at bargain prices. Advertisements offer simple, uncontested divorces for an apparently low rate.

The clinics usually charge a modest initial fee for a consultation with a lawyer who explains the alternatives and quotes a range of fees.

Storefront lawyers are usually young and can't command the high fees charged by more experienced attorneys. And clinic staffs are often more preponderantly composed of paralegals, who can take care of paperwork and other matters that don't require a lawyer. Most clinics have plain offices in low-rent districts or the suburbs.

Clinics are the K-mart of the legal profession and usually provide good service without the high overhead. Why pay for the fancy downtown offices of a traditional law firm? their proponents point out. A young lawyer may, in fact, devote more time to the case than an experienced attorney who has been through numerous similar cases.

Critics, on the other hand, claim that clinics can only make a profit if they deal in high volume, and this can mean that the storefront lawyer doesn't have enough time to give cases individual attention.

Moreover, the ads for "a simple, uncontested divorce" can be misleading. Often they attract clients who don't realize that their situation doesn't lend itself to such a divorce. The storefront lawyer will say their case is "a little more complicated" and quote an hourly rate that is close to the standard in the community.

Since most lawyers charge by the hour, the client should feel free to compare.

DO-IT-YOURSELF DIVORCES

Finally, a couple can divorce themselves. There's no law that says you have to have a lawyer in a divorce case.

The do-it-yourself approach applies only to that "simple, uncontested divorce." Generally speaking, it requires that the couple have only been married a short time, have no children, and can agree on how they want to divide their property.

Since divorce records are public property, the couple may look over copies of uncontested divorces on file at the county clerk's office to use as guidelines in writing up their own divorce agreement. Using legal terms isn't necessary.

Groups such as the National Organization of Women hold *pro se* divorce classes in some cities to show couples how to file the proper forms and represent themselves in court.

Divorce Yourself, based in New York City, sells kits with a worksheet the couple fills out and returns to them. The firm fills out the proper papers and processes them through the courts for a moderate fee.

Understandably, many attorneys warn against the do-it-yourself approach, especially for couples who are not aware of their legal rights. Even simple cases can involve issues too easily overlooked.

"Trained professionals are a fact of life," Richard Williams insists. "It's like saying you should go to a doctor for open-heart surgery but feel free to remove your own tonsils. How simple is simple?"

• • •

The experiences of Sara, Frank, Judy, and even Elizabeth illustrate how important it is to get the right lawyer in a divorce case.

Like most professionals today, lawyers tend to become specialists, and with the increased sophistication of the law it can be vitally important to hire a lawyer who is familiar with matrimonial statutes. Sara found a competent matrimonial lawyer through a friend who had been through a divorce. She could have asked the attorney who handled their house closing and wills to recommend a specialist in matrimonial law. She could have obtained the names of matrimonial lawyers through the local bar association or the American Association of Matrimonial Lawyers and made her own choice.

Perhaps more important, the stories prove how even matrimonial lawyers aren't cut from the same mold. The specialty has its share of straight businesslike types, others who take a personal interest, and, of course, hard-core barracudas. The choice should be a matter of personal preference.

The professional who goes to bed with a client falls into a special category, one to be avoided however great the need for "understanding." The lawyer who makes uninvited sexual advances should be reported to the bar association.

Frank's story shows how important it is for the client to communicate with the lawyer, to take part in making decisions and follow up when the agreement doesn't work out.

The person going through a divorce may feel too emotionally drained to participate. Sara realized, too late, that she would probably have benefited from professional counseling at the time of her divorce.

Lawyers have their responsibilities, but so have litigants. In a divorce situation, these include the following:

- Deciding when to hire a lawyer and getting the right lawyer for the case

- Compiling the vital statistics of both parties and their children, an inventory of property and other assets, insurance policies, wills, and other personal papers
- Preparing a budget and expected income
- Looking into the possibility of mediation or counseling if arguments aren't being settled and the process appears to be at a standstill
- Changing lawyers or getting a second opinion if the divorce agreement doesn't seem logical
- Following up if the agreement doesn't work out after the divorce is final

4: THE DYING MARRIAGE

"We considered divorce," Victoria Gish said. "But we didn't want to go through all the expense and paperwork."

Speaking in a precise British accent, Victoria was pouring strong tea into an eggshell-thin china cup. She glanced up. "Milk or sugar?"

Victoria had a flair for understatement, for getting directly to the point. Typically, she had dropped her comment on divorce without preamble. In fact, she had just been telling me that she and her husband had their thirty-seventh wedding anniversary coming up that week.

She passed the scones and curdled cream as soberly and precisely as a priest might serve bread and wine from the communion table.

"Howard and I have different interests, different values," she said, settling back in a deep chair, sipping her tea. "We have separate bank accounts, separate lives in many ways."

Her words contrasted sharply with the initial impression the couple presented to outsiders. In their mid-fifties with two grown children, the Gishes had moved from London about two years before to a stone cottage in Dorset overlooking the sea. This should have been the harvesttime of their marriage, the time to reap the rewards for years of work and raising a family.

"I didn't want to leave London," Victoria said. "I had a good position teaching children with learning disabilities. I had my own income. I felt needed and worthwhile. I had an identity."

As she talked about her marriage, Victoria looked thoughtfully out the wide, small-paned windows. Prematurely snow-white hair framed her face, still smooth and youthful-looking. She was dressed warmly in a blue wool jumper, white turtleneck sweater, and blue woolen stockings. The November air was chilly and the cottage had no central heating.

Despite the chill, red impatiens bloomed profusely in the stone urns on the terrace. Beyond the flagstone terrace, the land dropped sharply to the rocky cove formed by the sea. The steep inlet was a playground for seagulls, swooping and soaring in the wind.

"Howard was gone frequently while the children were growing up, and there were a lot of transfers," Victoria said. "Some women adapt to that and even enjoy it. I resented it."

The couple met in London, where Howard was spending his shore leave from the Royal Navy during World War II. They corresponded for almost a year before Howard proposed, and they were married shortly after.

"Those brief times together during the war were romantic, but I assumed we'd settle down and be a family when it was over," Victoria said. "I was shocked when Howard told me he had reenlisted and wanted to make the navy his career. He didn't even discuss it with me."

Victoria had moved dutifully, attempting to adjust to the life of a navy officer's wife. When Howard was assigned to a desk job in London, she thought they were finally settled in one place. Their children had left home and Victoria had resumed her teaching career. She had a new life.

When Howard announced he was being transferred to a remote area in southern England, Victoria said she refused to move.

"I stayed in London until we sold the house and Howard bought this place," she said. "I threatened to get a divorce and Howard told me to go ahead. He didn't want to talk about it."

Darkness came early in November. Victoria's voice was matter-of-fact and her expression was barely visible in the dusk. The lights of a ship could be seen on the horizon.

After a moment of silence, Victoria sighed and switched on the lamp by her chair. She began to place the tea things carefully on a tray.

"We can't afford the expense of a divorce," she said, and added with a smile, "And I'm a bit too old to go home to Mum."

By tacit agreement Victoria runs the house and prepares the meals. Howard keeps their cars in running order, makes repairs around the house, and takes care of the yardwork.

Howard goes to his favorite pub every evening after dinner to play skittles and drink bitters with his men friends.

Unable to get a regular teaching position, Victoria signed up for substitute teaching in the local schools. She works about half time, although the calls are irregular. She reads or watches television in the evening. The high point of her week is watching *Dynasty*, or *"Dinasty,"* as the British call it, on Thursday evenings. She goes to bed before Howard gets home from the pub, but sometimes she hears him laboring up the stairs, slowed down by a few too many pints of bitters.

IS IT REALLY SO SUDDEN?

The announcement of a divorce is often unexpected, sometimes shocking to the spouse who is suddenly told, "I want a divorce."

Yet common sense tells us that people rarely make major life decisions on the spur of the moment. Jim dropped his bombshell news on Sara almost as casually as he dropped the olive into his martini. But later he admitted to Sara that he had agonized over his decision for months. Like many people who make the decision to get a divorce, he had been discontented for some time.

In attempting to understand the circumstances that can lead to divorce, we came across studies that reveal some disconcerting facts about marriage. In *How's Your Family?* Dr. Jerry M. Lewis notes that almost half of all marriages now end in divorce, but he goes on to cite an even more alarming figure. Among couples who remain married, about half are "emotionally divorced," meaning they feel no real closeness or intimacy with their spouses.

Psychologists put these marriages into three categories—the devitalized, the passive congenial, and the conflict-habituated.

The devitalized marriage is the "life of quiet desperation" described by Thoreau. The couple once had intimacy and sharing, including at least an adequate sex life, but they stopped building the relationship. They now lack communication, shared goals, and sexual compatibility.

The Gishes tolerate a devitalized marriage because it's easier than going through "the expense and paperwork." As the Ericksons' divorce illustrates, if one of them meets a third party or there is some other triggering event, this could change.

In a passive congenial marriage, the couple can be comfortable despite the lack of intimacy and sharing. Their activities and interests are like their towels—marked his and hers. The marriage resembles the passive supportive marriage of the 1950s. Dad was pictured in the easy chair and Mom in the kitchen, the head and heart of the household respectively. Many couples still live that way and feel comfortable with it.

The Johnstons had a passive congenial marriage. Jim spent

every free evening and weekend on their boat. Sara had the housework, entertaining, and her part-time job. They were outwardly content until Jim began to look for "something more," as men at midlife sometimes do.

The conflict-habituated couple would "rather fight than switch." Although the marriage is strife ridden, if one partner dies or leaves, the other is grief stricken. It isn't easy to find a good battery mate.

A couple who had fought for years finally filed for divorce. The woman expressed a familiar lament through her tears. "I can't live with him, but I can't live without him." She lived, but the adjustment was difficult.

The ties that held these emotionally divorced couples together in past generations have, for the most part, been removed. Divorce is no longer a social stigma. Most religions have become more tolerant of divorce. Women have become more financially independent.

While most women probably know they could support themselves if necessary, economics may still be a factor that makes some couples hesitate to get a divorce, particularly among the middle class. The poor don't have much to lose and often walk away from a bad marriage. The wealthy can afford to keep up two or more households. But the middle class, who tend to center their life-style on money in the bank and material possessions such as a nice home, cars, vacations, or expensive hobbies, may be reluctant to risk losing the security and pleasures they've worked hard to attain.

A successful businessman listened to his friend's argument that, statistically, the chances of finding the right mate the first time or even second time around were slim. He countered: "What if each time you got a divorce your assets were divided in half? How long would you persevere in the search for the ideal mate?"

A bonding, or "attachment," makes it difficult for some people to end an unhappy marriage. In *Marital Separation*, sociologist Robert S. Weiss describes the erosion of love and the persistence of attachment.

"Even when marriages turn bad and the other components of love fade or turn into opposites, attachment is likely to remain," Weiss writes. He compares this to battered children who remain attached to their parents no matter how badly they're treated.

Dependency holds some couples together. One or both partners believe they really couldn't make it alone.

Religious beliefs also serve to hold some couples in unsatisfactory marriages. Although divorce is no longer considered a sin in most denominations, many couples still see marriage "for better or for worse," a lifetime commitment.

A beautiful French actress noted how Europeans place high values on titles and estates. She remarked, "If the marriage goes bad, it's more practical for the wife to take a lover and the husband to have a mistress."

CONTRIBUTING ATTITUDES

Mark Trowbridge listened to his wealthy men friends discuss their views on women and marriage, marveling at how flippant they appeared to be. Admittedly, Mark was sensitive about this issue. His wife had died only a few months before after eight years of fighting cancer.

The southwestern regional manager for a major corporation, Mark had immersed himself in his work since her death. "My work is my life," he stated matter-of-factly. His only social life was business-related. Entertaining business associates was a necessity, and it was important that he, in turn, accept their hospitality. A day of deer and boar hunting at a business associate's Texas ranch, for example, had become an annual event.

Mark felt tired and surprisingly drained as he relaxed with his companions at the end of the day, warmed by the finest bourbon whiskey and a roaring fire in the Texas-size fireplace.

"You guys should have seen the one he missed," his host taunted good-naturedly. "If it had been any closer, he could have reached out and pulled its tail."

The conversation was typical of these gatherings, moving from their hits and misses that day to the chances the Dallas Cowboys would make the playoffs, predictions on how the president's budget would affect the economy, the sorry state of the beef market. By the third or fourth drink, the men became philosophical.

Mark was well acquainted with the five men gathered around the fire. The youngest, Al Harper, was probably in his late thirties. The oldest, Ben Richards, was in his mid-fifties. Despite the wide range in ages, the men shared similar values. Mark knew that each of them had long since passed the millionaire mark, and each relished the freedom and life-style his wealth provided. The talk had now turned, as it often did, to women and marriage.

"If we're only going to pass this way once, the woman we live with should be the one who is the most pleasing to us," Ben Richards said. "To work hard on a less than satisfactory relationship is dumb."

Smiles and nods around the fireplace circle proved at least some of the men agreed with him. Jim Blaine, who had recently remarried for the third time, spoke up next.

"He's right," Jim said. "There are just too many good-looking, entertaining, and available women to settle for less than first class."

Aware of his approving audience, Ben warmed to his subject. "Which one of us would keep a house, a car, or anything else we didn't fully like? Then why should we endure a less than satisfactory relationship in the most important part of our daily life—the woman we're married to?"

Not wanting to reveal the dull ache this conversation was arousing in his gut, Mark spoke up for the first time. "I'm not sure you can compare a wife with the latest-model car," he said quietly. "After all, you don't own a wife."

Ben shook his head adamantly. "You don't get my point. I'm saying a wife has the same right to make the best of her life. Is the quality of her life, the frame of reference for the family, better off in an inferior relationship?"

Ben had made a good point, and the others obviously agreed with him. They could afford the best, including the latest-model wife. Mark sipped his drink, wondering idly if their former wives would agree and how their trade-in value had been determined.

This candid fireside conversation among wealthy and powerful businessmen illustrates a paradox of the 1980s. People seem to expect more out of their marriages but appear less willing to make an investment. Couples go into marriage with high expectations. Yet they don't put much into the marriage, and they depend less on the marriage for their total happiness.

The quality of life is enhanced by good relationships, the men seem to be saying, and most people would agree. The wife has the same right to make the most of her life, Ben argues, also reflecting the philosophy of the 1980s. Women are no longer asked to accommodate men, as they were in the 1960s. Women are no longer asked to put on their white boots and baby-doll pajamas before greeting their men at the door as Marabel Morgan advocated in *The Total Woman*. The watchword for the 1980s is "identity," and both men and women seek it.

These privileged men appeared to be unaware of the step beyond personal identity when one can choose to make a commitment to a partnership, group, or community. The decision to compromise oneself willingly can also enhance the quality of life they prize so highly.

Cars wear out and the old model gets traded in. Marriage

partners change, and the couple must decide, Do we retool or trade in? Are we mature enough to cope with the changes? Can we resolve the questions and differences we face?

Mark thought about his own marriage. His wife, Connie, had been an artist who had never really understood the demands of business. On the other hand, Mark hadn't always taken to the artistic types she had brought into their home. But somehow they had faced and muddled through life's crises with love and humor.

He thought about his friends. In their eagerness to grab the gusto, weren't they missing something else?

THE MISSING INGREDIENT

They're called Yuppies. They grew up in the "me" generation, determined to change the world and achieve self-actualization. While some of their cohorts became disillusioned, the Yuppies put on three-piece suits when they came of age and succeeded by adopting the material values they once rejected.

Anne and Philip Hartley epitomize the Yuppie generation—young, upwardly mobile, ambitious. They met while both were getting their master's degrees in business. By their mid-thirties, they were both on the fast track in their careers and traveling first class.

In view of that, Anne's comment on her marriage was startling.

"I've got an eighty-percent marriage," she said.

Anne was the business planner for a unit of a large aerospace company in Los Angeles. Her husband, Philip, was in line for a vice-presidency in an elite consulting firm's West Coast office. Their apartment near Anne's office in Century City, a stone's throw from Beverly Hills, was elegant. The white plush carpeting and soft earth-tone walls provided the perfect backdrop for their custom-designed modern furniture.

What was missing?

"I'm almost thirty-four," Anne said as she poured Perrier water into tall glasses and added a twist of lemon. "Suddenly I've got this giant drive inside of me to have a baby. I'm getting close to the cut-off point for childbearing. If I don't do it soon, I never will."

This wasn't the first time I'd heard a woman in her thirties express that "giant drive." Is there something in the female makeup that kicks into gear when the end of the childbearing years is in view? Women who already have children, who thought their family was complete, have decided on "just one more" baby during that crucial last-ditch period.

"The problem is, Phil doesn't want any part of it," Anne said. "When we got married, we agreed we didn't want to have a family, and he won't let me forget that. He says he won't be tied down. He likes the freedom to make a weekend trip to Baja or fly to London when we get a few days off to shop and see the shows."

Anne didn't look like a woman yearning for motherhood. Her white linen suit with its loosely fitted jacket and black silk blouse looked like a Ralph Lauren. Her dark blond hair was swept back in a layered style, and her makeup had the natural look that professional makeup artists teach. But her deep-set blue eyes were troubled.

"I've tried to figure out why I've changed," she said, speaking slowly. "I think it probably comes down to wanting fulfillment. Maybe the only true fulfillment for a woman is having a child."

After a thoughtful silence, Anne spoke again. "I've considered stopping the birth control pills and running the risk that Phil would feel differently when he saw a child of his own. But that scenario seemed so dishonest, I couldn't live with it."

Anne said she woke up every morning and went to bed every night wrestling with the same questions. Should she settle for an 80-percent marriage? Or should she leave Phil and hope she meets a man who wants children before time runs out?

Surprising as it may seem, marriages that appear to be strong in all other ways often break up over a single unresolved issue. In this case, the issue was important to Anne, and she had reached an impasse in trying to resolve it with her husband.

About two months later, Anne called to say she was in the area on business and would like to meet for dinner.

We had barely greeted each other and given the waiter our cocktail order when Anne made her announcement.

"I've left him," she said, her mouth quivering, tears streaming down her face.

Anne's friends and relatives would puzzle over why a woman who seemingly had everything would give it all up with the vague explanation that "there's got to be more." If anything, Anne was a few years behind schedule. Women who have achieved intimacy in their marriage and satisfaction in their careers often move into a "generative" stage around the age of twenty-eight to thirty. They want a child.

In a sense, Anne's story is a variation on the familiar big sister–little sister theme. One sister gets married, settles in a small town, and has a family. The other sister goes off to win fame and fortune in Hollywood, New York, or you name it. They meet, and each is acutely aware of the emptiness of life. There's got to be more.

Men go through a similar stage later, usually in their forties when they've reached the mentoring stage in their careers. They come to the same conclusion: "There's got to be more."

Sara's husband, Jim, felt it so strongly that he gave up a successful career and a twenty-six-year marriage to pursue it. People often ask about their friends, "Why are they getting a divorce now after staying together for all those years?" This is often the answer.

Now Anne, despite her tears, had found the quest for "more" irresistible.

A DOUBLE LIFE

The wheels of the plane hit the landing strip at the Boston airport, and the rough thud seemed to crystallize the feelings of doubt that had been running through Debbie Matheson's thoughts.

She should not have come to visit her parents right now. It was too soon after her divorce.

Debbie had tried writing her parents a lengthy letter, hoping she could explain why divorce was the only solution to a brief marriage that had been a bad match from the start. The words had seemed too cold and logical. A marriage is too deeply personal, the relationship too multifaceted to explain to any outsider. In the end, Debbie had ripped up the letter and picked up the telephone.

Her father's immediate reaction had been typical.

"Why don't you come home?"

Home. A comforting thought. But this was not a scraped knee or a case of summer camp homesickness.

"I've got a job," she'd reminded him.

When Debbie had told her mother, the response was more emotional and the two women had ended up fighting tears.

"Thanks for not saying 'I told you so,'" Debbie had said before they'd hung up.

Her mother would have had every right to point this out, Debbie thought. She had warned her, expressing her concern as openly and kindly as possible. "You haven't known each other very long," she had said. "Don't you think it would be wise to put it off a bit?"

That word of warning had made Debbie even more determined to go ahead with her plans. She had met George on a ski weekend in Vermont, and it had been love at first sight.

True, they had only known each other for three months, but what did time have to do with it? Once her parents had realized Debbie wasn't going to change her mind, they'd come through, as always. They had flown to Atlanta for the small wedding and taken the bridal party to dinner. They had been charming, gracious. Debbie had been proud of them.

But dammit, her mother had been right. Debbie had known it almost immediately. Why was her mother always right? Debbie loved her mother, but in a peculiar way, she resented her. Debbie had never felt she could quite measure up.

Emerging from the gate, Debbie spotted her parents a split second before they saw her. Her father, towering above the crowd, looked distinguished with his silvery hair and black cashmere topcoat. Her mother, Sally, petite and matronly, wore a short mink jacket over a bright red suit.

"Debbie!"

Debbie's mother hugged her warmly. Her father, taking her ticket stubs, went off to get the baggage.

"We have tickets for the symphony tomorrow night, and the Randolphs have invited us all to a party on Saturday," Sally said as soon as they were settled in the car. "But this is your weekend. We want to do exactly what you want to do."

Not a word about Debbie's divorce during the drive home or the dinner. Debbie might have been on a break from college, asking about old friends, hearing news of the latest engagements, marriages, and babies.

"I hope you weren't too upset about the divorce," Debbie said later as they finished their coffee in the living room.

"Just sorry," Sally said. "How do you feel about it? That's the important thing."

Debbie shook her head. "I'm fine. I feel like I did a pretty stupid thing."

Debbie's father put down his coffee cup. "If you girls will excuse me, I've got some work to do."

For as long as Debbie could remember, her father had gone

into his den after dinner to work for several hours before bedtime, often joining them again for the eleven o'clock news. She had always assumed all men gave their work top priority. What a shock it had been to find out her own husband had apparently no desire to succeed. His ambition, as nearly as Debbie could judge, had been to spend as much time as possible on the ski slopes.

"You didn't do anything stupid," Sally said as she came back into the room carrying a carafe of sherry and two glasses. "We're all human. We all make mistakes."

"The stupid part was assuming I'd have a marriage like you and Dad," Debbie said. "You've always been the perfect couple. I don't think I ever heard you have an argument."

Sally sipped her sherry, watching her daughter thoughtfully.

"Debbie," she said. "I think there's something I should tell you. I don't think there are many perfect marriages if you scratch the surface impressions people make. I've had to solve my own problem of a less than perfect marriage with . . . what you might call . . . another relationship."

Debbie couldn't quite grasp what her mother was saying.

"An affair?"

"Well, I suppose it started out that way," Sally said, carefully selecting her words. "But I don't think it qualifies as an affair anymore, not after almost twenty years."

Debbie was dumbfounded. Twenty years!

"Who is it?" Recovering quickly, Debbie added, "I'm sorry. That's none of my business."

"I don't mind," Sally said placidly, refilling her glass. "Do you remember Joe Evans?"

Joe Evans. Dr. Joseph Evans. He was the family internist and friend. They had belonged to the same country club. Debbie recalled the quiet, likable man, hardly her idea of a Lothario.

"We met once a week in his office for years," Sally said.

"I was too healthy to justify that many trips to the doctor, so I had to develop my chronic sinus problem."

Debbie heard the words, but she couldn't believe what her mother was saying. "Did you ever think of leaving Dad?"

"Not seriously," Sally said quickly. "I love your father and I wouldn't do anything to hurt him. I just had to accept the fact that we have different physical and emotional needs. If anything, I think my relationship with Joe has helped me become more understanding, more compassionate in all my relationships with people. I don't demand as much as I used to. I can be more accepting, more content."

Debbie was beginning to grasp the picture. She, too, had felt the austere quality in her father. She loved and admired him, but she had often wondered if he ever let anyone get really close to him.

Sally had pulled her knees up under her on the couch. Her arm lay across the backrest, the sherry glass held loosely in her hand. Why had her mother revealed such a personal, human side of herself?

"You're hard on yourself sometimes, Debbie," Sally said. "Don't beat yourself to death over this divorce. It's difficult. Life is difficult sometimes."

They talked, growing drowsy from the sherry. Debbie told her mother about the letter she had tried to write, how hard it had been to put her feelings about the divorce into words. Sally shared some funny stories about her thwarted attempts to see Joe while he was recuperating from a gall bladder operation and couldn't go to the office. They had finally gotten away for a drive in the country one afternoon.

"We were talking away and Joe drove off the road and right into a ditch," Sally said. "Talk about panic. I was sure someone we knew would drive by, so we both ducked down on the front seat every time a car went by. Finally a truck driver pulled up and asked if we needed some help. He must have thought we were crazy. Anyway, he pulled the car out and I insisted on driving home."

They talked until Debbie's father came into the room, stretching and yawning.

"Mind if I turn on the eleven o'clock news?"

Their next evenings together, the three of them went to the symphony and to the Randolphs' party. Debbie found herself watching her parents. She could see the mutual respect between them. She wondered if her mother had made the most workable compromise. The weekend passed quickly, however, and there was no more time for talk.

"Thanks," Debbie said as she kissed her parents good-bye at the airport. Glancing at her mother, she added, "For everything."

Debbie had asked the stewardess for a pillow, but now she couldn't sleep. The implications of her mother's revelation troubled her.

As a youngster, Debbie had assumed her family life was fairly typical, as measured against the ideal families on *Leave It to Beaver* and *Father Knows Best*. Mothers were supposed to be pretty, soft-spoken, and incredibly patient. Fathers were wise, not only in their professions but in solving family problems. Parents related to each other with affection, but not sexually. Arguments were limited to such matters as a teenager who wanted the car. They never fought.

Although Debbie's image of marriage had been modified by growing older and her decision to have a career, she had assumed her marriage would have the solid, stable qualities she had admired in her parents' relationship. By comparison, George had been an overgrown spoiled child.

While it was comforting to know her mother was less than perfect, the disclosure of the affair was also disquieting. Her marriage model had been shattered. In a sense, her mother was just as "divorced" as she.

Several years ago, columnist Ann Landers was asked if she had ever considered divorce.

"No," she said. "Murder, yes. Divorce, no."

Sadly, she did have to think about it a few years later when her marriage came apart. She wrote movingly about the experience in her columns, a reminder to millions of readers that no one is immune.

Surely almost every married couple has thought about divorce at one time or another during particularly stressful and difficult times. It isn't easy to spend a lifetime with a person of the opposite sex, particularly if the initial attraction is based more on physical than other, more enduring attributes. A cartoon in *Psychology Today* depicts a middle-aged man confronting his frowsy wife with a wedding photograph as she is frying eggs.

"Who are you and what have you done with the girl in this wedding photo?!"

What happens to a couple from the time they joyfully pose for the wedding photograph and the day they announce their divorce?

One of the first signs of a failing marriage is a sense of emptiness, a void. Tender touching and loving behavior stops. The unspoken feeling of intimacy disappears. The spontaneous telephone call, the thoughtful gestures stop. And the laughter stops.

"We went out to dinner the other night and I realized we were both tense, taking everything we talked about so seriously," one man said. "We used to enjoy each other's company. We used to have fun."

Unable to resolve basic issues, such as how to raise their children and set common goals, the couple gradually backs away from true communication. Conversations usually begin to center on trivial matters and maintenance issues.

When this happens, the marriage is for the most part emotionally dead. While the decision to divorce may come later, or even be postponed indefinitely, the couple is emotionally divorced. As Dennis Boike puts it, "The marriage is all over except for the time frame."

5: SOCIALLY SINGLE

The dinner parties, ski trips, weekends at a lake cottage, the Saturday night dances, or casual summer cookouts, all the special events that make up a married couple's social life usually end abruptly when one's marriage partner is gone.

The loss of social contact with old friends is particularly painful for the widowed because we, as a society, try so hard to convince the bereaved that nothing will change. They are to be supported. Friends rally around with flowers and hot dishes, assuring the newly widowed they will always be there. "Just call if you need anything—anything." The attention barely outlasts the flowers and food, perhaps a few weeks.

Even when friends make an effort to stay in touch, the newly single person often feels out of place with the friends they knew as a couple, like the proverbial "fifth wheel," and sometimes old friends see the single person as a potential threat. The suddenly single is suddenly "available." The best friend's husband who offers his "services" is not a myth, single women say.

Loneliness forces most single people to seek companionship

fairly soon. Studies indicate that more than half of separated people have begun dating by the end of the first year and almost all by the end of the second year.

As the divorce rate rises to almost 50 percent, the formerly married are finding some stunning changes in traditional social customs. Although men still do most of the asking, the traditional "date" is almost extinct, especially among younger singles. The proliferation of singles bars and clubs, singles cruises and ski trips, health clubs and spas is a response to the growing number of singles in their twenties, thirties, and forties who are looking for new ways to meet other single people.

Dating and escort services advertise everything from a companion for an evening out in a strange city to matchmaking for a permanent relationship.

The singles themselves seem to feel more free to take the direct approach. Advertising in newspapers and magazines for "companionship" or "a possible lasting relationship," once carried by underground newspapers, is now commonplace in reputable newspapers and magazines. "Having recently become available, I don't want to waste time," read a succinct advertisement in a major regional magazine.

The visible singles who crowd into bars and sign up for cruises are, for the most part, urban singles who are free to choose their own life-style. Millions of formerly married suburbanites, however, are choosing to stay in the suburbs, where they are often isolated in a social structure geared for pairs.

Singles who were married for many years may wonder what has happened to the rules for social behavior. There's no one "right way" for a single person to behave in the 1980s. Women today have the freedom to take the initiative in a relationship. Couples who choose to live together before marriage are accepted in most communities. Sex before marriage is generally assumed.

This new freedom can be an exciting challenge to the natural adventurer. But most people feel threatened, even frightened by the lack of rules.

TO BED OR NOT TO BED

Striking changes in moral values force the formerly married to reexamine feelings and attitudes about their own sexuality.

"The last time I dated was in college, and there was at least the assumption your virginity was at stake," Judy Carpenter said. "Now every man I meet seems to think I'm sexually frustrated."

Despite her confused feelings after her divorce and the brief, hapless affair with her lawyer, Judy started dating again within a few weeks.

"Our social life had revolved entirely around Steve's students and friends on the faculty," Judy said. "I was good at charming the dean or an important visitor to the campus. I had enjoyed that, and I missed it."

Judy's social life ended as soon as she and Stephen separated. "I went to a few parties with friends, but I felt like an outsider. I didn't expect that in a college town because we have several single faculty members. Then it hit me. Every time one of the men started talking to me or asked me to dance, I'd feel like his wife was glaring at me."

Although Judy had wanted the divorce, she felt insecure and rejected after Stephen packed his clothes and went to Santa Barbara to accept a visiting professorship.

The affair with her lawyer, a temporary boost to Judy's self-esteem, left her feeling even more rejected. When the pressure built up, she would go on a drinking binge.

Feeling her life was getting out of control, Judy decided to move to New York City the summer after her divorce was final. The move, Judy thought, would be a fresh start. A friend from college had offered the use of her apartment while she was away on vacation. Judy would have time to find her own place and look for a job.

Under the joint custody agreement, Kristen would stay with Stephen in Boulder for the rest of the summer and join Judy in New York in time to enroll in school that fall.

Judy felt euphoric during her first few days in New York City. Her friend's Greenwich Village apartment was small but comfortable. She strolled through the neighborhood smiling at strangers. She delighted in eating alone at a neighborhood restaurant where they served delicious Spanish food at reasonable prices. The paella was dished out from a battered pan and served with an icy pitcher of sangria.

After a week of fruitless job hunting and checking out apartments that were already rented or out of her price range, Judy's insecurities began to resurface. She was lonely. The heat was becoming oppressive. The mental images of Stephen frolicking with a series of pretty young graduate students and charging it all to Visa added to her misery.

"I ended up going to bed with the first man who showed an interest in me," Judy said. "I had met him in the bar at the airport and given him my telephone number. I was thrilled when he called me. The relationship was great for my ego . . . until I found out he was married."

As the time came for her friend Dorothy to return from vacation, Judy became increasingly depressed. She hadn't found a job or an apartment. Kristen would be arriving in a few weeks.

"I've made a mess of everything," Judy confessed to Dorothy tearfully.

The sight of Judy blinking back tears from her wide blue eyes aroused her friend's sympathy.

"You've got to stay here," Dorothy insisted. "You can sleep on the couch."

Dorothy regretted the impulsive invitation the first time she brought a friend home and found Judy already asleep on the living room couch. She began to take a personal interest in helping Judy find a job and an apartment.

Through Dorothy's contacts, Judy finally got a job as an assistant at a publishing house and found a two-bedroom apartment in Queens near the high school Kristen would be attending.

Judy was barely settled in her new apartment when Kristen arrived in late August. The landlord hadn't come through with his promise of new blinds for the bedrooms, and Judy hadn't found time to iron the curtains, but she did her best to make Kristen's arrival special. She found fresh red snapper at the corner market and carefully followed Craig Claiborne's recipe in the *New York Times*. She bought a bouquet of flowers from a vendor to brighten the table.

Kristen was polite but uncommunicative during the first few weeks. She missed her friends and the casual, outdoor life of Boulder. She was finding it difficult to adjust to the new school. A rift began to develop between mother and daughter.

"For one thing, the neighbors assumed we were sisters, and that created a problem," Judy recalled. "Kristen was just discovering her sexuality, and in some ways I was going through exactly the same thing. I was trying to take the attitude that sex isn't a big deal, that I really needed to experiment. But when I suspected Kristen of experimenting, believe me, it was a big deal."

Kristen was growing into a beautiful young woman. She had inherited her mother's striking red hair, and her small figure was beginning to develop. Although Kristen seemed unaware of her beauty, Judy was more than aware of the glances her daughter attracted from men.

Judy's sense of becoming an outsider among her old friends was quite real, but she was only picking up part of the message. The glances of the faculty wives told Judy she represented a sexual threat. Judy would have been surprised to know that she was even more threatening as an "ideas resource," as Dennis Boike calls it, for the frustrated married women among the faculty crowd. The newly divorced often appear to be leading an enviable life. So, while the wives cast their jealous glances, more than one of their husbands wondered, "Is my wife getting ideas?" Judy didn't have a chance.

Judy's short-lived euphoria in New York City was normal and predictable. Security is quite tenuous at this stage without the support of a significant "other person." Judy's resentment of what her ex-husband was doing, or might be doing, was a normal, quite common response.

Trying to convince herself that sex is "not a big deal" was an attempt at self-deception. More often than not, sex *is* a big deal.

While it's true that women now have sexual freedom, how many feel comfortable about using their newly found freedom? Judy was still experimenting.

"MEAT MARKETS"

Judy's "pickup" in an airport bar had happened by chance, but today's single bar scene often seems like the first logical place to meet other singles. Although the growing fear of contracting AIDS or herpes has made singles more cautious about casual sex, the hunt goes on.

"They really are meat markets," Debbie Matheson said. "The guys move in on their prey toward the end of the evening, investing as little interest, time, and money as possible to score."

Debbie, an attractive thirty-one-year-old Atlanta businesswoman, exudes confidence, but she admitted she didn't feel confident after her divorce.

"Whatever the reason for the divorce, you feel totally rejected, and that's hard to handle. Right away I took a guy home and seduced him. Then I couldn't get him to leave. For a whole year, he was just always there. It's my apartment and I should have maintained control. I lost it on my first fling."

Resilient. The word kept coming to mind as Debbie talked about her adjustments after her divorce. As the daughter of a wealthy Boston family, Debbie had grown up in a sheltered environment. She could easily have graduated from being "Daddy's girl" to becoming the pampered wife of any number of young men in her social circle. Her blond hair, flawless complexion, and unassuming manner had attracted men the way bees are attracted to flowers.

Debbie was also intelligent. After graduating cum laude from an eastern women's college, she had joined a stock brokerage firm that was expanding into new investment areas. Debbie's willingness to work long hours and her valuable suggestions quickly paid off in a raise and a promotion.

Debbie met George on a ski weekend in Vermont, and they were married three months later. Unfortunately, the delightful compatibility they had shared on the ski slopes didn't carry over to everyday life. George didn't share Debbie's enthusiasm for her work or her ambition to get ahead. Within a few months, Debbie had concluded George was lazy.

Seated in her office, Debbie appeared feminine and businesslike in a dress-for-success black suit and rose silk scarf. Her hairstyle was neat and uncluttered—straight blond hair that turned under slightly above the shoulder. Her voice was soft but projected complete self-assurance.

"I met some men in bars who were completely tactless," she said. Smiling slightly, she ran over the standard questions of a typical opening gambit in a singles bar:

"Do you come here often?"
"Where do you work?"
"Do you have children?"

"Do you live alone?"

"Where do you live?"

The last question is the real clincher, Debbie said with a certain bitterness. "Contrary to popular belief, a man will not follow you to the ends of the earth. The town line would be more like it."

After that first year with the man who came to dinner and wouldn't go home, Debbie grew more cautious about becoming involved.

"I learned to celebrate the temporary," she said. "Even the brief encounter, a casual conversation over a cup of coffee in a diner with someone you enjoy, can be a boost to your shattered self-esteem. I found myself able to enjoy a lover for a week or one night."

Although she was more popular than most divorced women, Debbie said she rarely had a real date.

"The day of calling ahead and making a date is almost extinct," she said. "If someone really interesting called on short notice, I went. Why pretend?"

Debbie said she tried to be honest and straightforward, but she soon learned some men don't share those values. Singles bars are the ideal place for married men on the prowl to meet available women who may be willing to settle for a brief affair with no questions asked.

But that wasn't for Debbie, who quickly learned some of the ways to spot married men. If they were never available on weekends and gave her an excuse when she asked for their home telephone number, she assumed they were married and refused to see them again.

She had no reason to suspect Don Allen when a business associate introduced them. Don was good-looking, thirty-three, and new in the area. He gave Debbie his telephone number, a hotel where he was staying until he found a place to live in Atlanta.

"I was falling head over heels in love with him," Debbie

said, recalling how she decided to surprise Don with tickets to a play and a late dinner at her apartment with candles, flowers, and wine.

When the operator at his hotel told her Don had checked out, Debbie decided to try his office.

An impersonal voice told her Don wasn't in and asked if she cared to leave a message. Feeling a sudden wave of disappointment, Debbie asked if she could have his new home number.

"He isn't there, but his wife may be."

Debbie stared at the telephone.

His wife?

"I was incensed," Debbie said. "He not only had a wife, but three children. And the woman who introduced us knew that! I couldn't believe a woman I'd considered a friend could do that to me. Needless to say, I have one less friend."

Angry and disappointed, Debbie gathered up the clothes Don had left in her apartment and wrapped them in a neat package. She addressed them to Don at his home address, enclosing a terse note:

"I'm sure you'll understand why I didn't wash your clothes this time."

The experience made her even more determined to be her own, more independent person, Debbie told me.

"I noticed a good-looking man in a bar the other night and I sent him a drink," Debbie said. "Why not? Men need reinforcement, too."

Debbie has had several marriage proposals, but, she said, "Married you can always get. Most of them are either insecure or on the rebound from another relationship."

We found this same, almost disdainful tone surfacing in numerous interviews with singles who make most of their social contacts in bars.

The attitude seemed to be: "Where else can we go?"

• • •

Singles bars can be a good place to meet other singles if a casual relationship is what you're seeking.

The problem with the singles bar—as with the health club, which is replacing the bar for singles who feel more relaxed about striking up casual conversation after a workout than over a drink—is in the expectations. When a single person goes into a bar or signs up for a club expecting to meet prospective dates or likely candidates for marriage, he or she is usually destined for frustration.

This sense of frustration and tension can be felt at any gathering of singles where dating is the main goal. The newly single need friends, people they enjoy for more than just physical gratification.

But singles bars and health clubs aren't the only alternatives.

SINGLES GROUPS

The first time Richard Morrison went to a dance sponsored by a singles club, he couldn't go through the door.

"I had to take two shots at it," Richard said. "I went back to my car and sat there for a while. Finally, I forced myself to go back in. I kept having the feeling that I was still married and didn't belong there."

Women outnumbered the men at the dance by about two to one, and Richard found that this made him feel even more uncomfortable.

"The women were all so friendly and so eager to please, I felt sorry for them. I kept thinking it was so obvious why we were all there. It was like announcing to the world that we were all a bunch of losers with no friends."

But sitting at home alone every night was worse, Richard finally concluded. When he received an invitation to a singles party a few months later, he decided to go. This time, the party was a clambake at the beach and the atmosphere was more casual, less intimidating than the dance.

"I'm trying to change my attitude," Richard said. "Sure, I've met a few losers in the group, just like any group. But I've met some nice people who go for the same reason I do. They're lonely. We don't talk about it a lot, but I know they understand what I'm going through."

A support group can be the first positive step toward rebuilding a social life. The newly single person needs friends, especially friends who empathize.

Parents Without Partners and Theos for the widowed are national groups with chapters in local communities. Churches often sponsor groups, such as Divorced and Separated Catholics. Single people have taken the initiative in many communities, forming small discussion groups for people just coming out of a divorce or unhappy with their experiences in social clubs.

The newly single person should avoid a group if the purpose seems to be mating up the members or the atmosphere is one of enjoying mutual misery.

Marriage therapists and professional counselors are usually aware of the effective, positive groups in a particular community. The Widowed Persons Service, based in Washington, D.C., can put the widowed in touch with possible local resources.

OTHER SOCIAL OPPORTUNITIES

Sports or hobbies may be temporarily forgotten during the mourning period. The skis gather dust. The sweater remains unfinished. Even reading may take too much energy.

At some point, resuming an old interest or taking up something new can open up a new social life.

Mark Trowbridge disdained the suggestion of joining a support group during our first interview. A lean, white-haired man of fifty-three, Mark had immersed himself in his work in the two years since his wife died of cancer.

"My work is my life," Mark said. "My wife was in charge of our social life. She was an artist, and she brought a lot of interesting people into our home. Without her, I had no reason to keep in contact with that circle."

Asked if he had considered a support group, Mark shook his head.

"Definitely not. That sort of thing wouldn't interest me."

He was equally adamant in his attitude about dating. "I've escorted women I know professionally on some occasions and enjoyed some pleasant evenings. But dating? No. I have no interest."

As an afterthought, he added, "That isn't to say there aren't times when I would like to have a woman in my bed. You get that itch."

Mark wasn't thinking about a social life when he signed up for a course in photography about six months later. He wanted to learn how to take better pictures.

The teacher was a free-lance photographer, Jennifer Moore, a woman in her late thirties whose work had appeared in several national magazines. Almost immediately, Mark and Jenny became friends.

Although Mark insists they're all business in the darkroom, they've gone on shooting expeditions together and with other members of the class. Without consciously seeking companionship, Mark soon had a small circle of friends outside of his work who shared his interest in photography.

Not every person who signs up for a course in photography ends up with an attractive teacher and a socially congenial group. Many singles have negative experiences.

"I joined a tennis club, but they put me in a class with some young people," said a widow in her fifties. "I mean young—in their twenties. Talk about feeling like a senior citizen!"

She stopped going and lost her membership fee. Later she regretted she had not been more assertive. She could have asked to change classes or invited someone her age to play.

The widow's experience is typical. Under the pressure of friends to "get out more" and "join in," the widowed and divorced may push themselves into awkward situations. And with their self-esteem so fragile, their ability to use common sense on their own so marginal, they withdraw at the first sign of rejection or failure. Later, in a more logical frame of mind, they look back on a trail of lost memberships and half-finished projects. The problem is usually one of expecting too much too soon.

Mark was kinder to himself and more patient. He waited until he was interested in taking the photography course, and he had one expectation—to take better pictures. Even if he hadn't met Jennifer or made new friends in his class, he wouldn't have complained: his pictures did improve.

SEXUAL EXPERIMENTATION

"If she's thinking romantic thoughts while he's mapping out the shortest route to the bed, forget the romance," Judy Carpenter said.

The small bar on Fifty-fourth Street was warm and cozy on a snowy afternoon. Judy and some of her friends from work had stopped off for a drink after work, and someone in the crowd introduced her to Jim Braden.

"We sat there talking after the others had left, and I found myself sharing feelings I hadn't shared with anyone," Judy said. "I didn't want it to end, so I asked Jim home to dinner."

When Jim suddenly discovered he didn't have any money, Judy paid for their drinks.

"He was even at ease with Kristen, asking her about her school and her interests. Kristen went to a friend's house after dinner to study for a test, and Jim helped me with the dishes. We made love, and I don't think I've ever felt so close to anyone, so in tune."

Judy was starry-eyed the next morning at work. Her starry eyes became troubled as the days passed and Jim didn't call her.

Kristen noticed how edgy her mother had become. "Is anything wrong?" she asked.

Judy shook her head. She didn't want her daughter to know how naive she had been.

Judy waited a week before she finally called Jim.

"He was the perfect gentleman," Judy said. "He told me he was looking forward to seeing me again and promised to call me soon to set up a lunch. He still hasn't called, of course."

The encounter shattered Judy's confidence in her judgment.

"I paid for his drinks with my child support money," Judy said. "I feel like a fool. First the fiasco with Matt and now this. Are all men obsessed by sex?"

Obsessed? Probably not. But most men do think a lot about sex, and to most men sex is ego enhancing and not necessarily equated with love.

The same can be said for women at this stage of low self-esteem. The woman needs to prove she's desirable.

Sexual experimentation occurs on three levels—for oneself, for the temporary relationship, and finally, for intimacy or a committed relationship. Judy was probably still on the first level but not feeling too comfortable about it. She used the term "made love."

Women have been told, either directly or indirectly, that sex without love or intimacy is wrong. If Judy had understood her need to experiment, she might have been more forgiving of herself. If she had taken a more realistic viewpoint of her evening with Jim, perhaps she could have accepted it as an enjoyable evening. Intimate relationships aren't formed in an evening, except in 1950s movies.

DATING AGAIN AT MIDDLE AGE

A date. Even the word amused Laura Cunningham. She shut the bathroom door self-consciously and plugged in her hair dryer.

This is so silly, she thought, studying her reflection in the bathroom mirror—a plain, pleasant-looking woman of fifty-two with laugh lines around her eyes and a stomach she could no longer suck in.

What on earth am I doing?

Laura had been alone for almost two years when Ben Johnson, a man she met through a mutual friend, asked her out to dinner. She had accepted, almost gratefully. Her husband, David, had been a homebody who liked to read and putter around the house. But now and then they had gone out to dinner or to a movie, and they had enjoyed playing bridge with a few close friends. Laura missed that. She had tried going out to dinner alone and had kept in touch with some of the women they had known by inviting them to go shopping or have lunch. It wasn't the same.

Laura carefully curled her short brown hair and slipped into a navy-blue dress.

"Dowdy." She took off the dress and hung it away.

She looked through her closet, realizing she hadn't bought anything new since David had died. Sighing, she picked out a light blue crepe she had bought for their son's wedding. David had thought she looked nice in it, she remembered wistfully. She could recall happy memories now without feeling pain.

"I felt so foolish getting all dressed up for a man I hardly knew," Laura said. "David and I were married for over twenty-five years, but I felt as nervous and unsure of myself as a teenager."

Laura's daughter Marcie seemed pleased that her mother was going out. She hurried to answer the door when the bell rang.

"It was awkward for everyone," Laura said. "I even forgot to let Ben hold my coat for me."

A stocky man with thinning gray hair, Ben had obviously taken pains to look his best in a conservative gray suit, white shirt, and maroon club tie.

This was something new for Ben, too, Laura realized, feeling a wave of empathy. When Ben asked her if she would like to try a new restaurant known for its good seafood and piano bar, Laura tried to sound enthusiastic as she replied, "Fine."

"That seemed to be the only word in my vocabulary," Laura said with a shake of her head. "The weather was fine. The food was fine. The music was fine. I felt like an idiot."

After dinner Ben asked Laura to dance, and finally she was beginning to relax and enjoy herself. She was smiling and talkative as they walked across the graveled parking lot to the car.

"You're very pretty when you smile," Ben said as he unlocked the car door.

Laura was pleased, touched by the compliment, and she smiled at Ben as he got into the driver's seat. Suddenly he moved toward her and tried to put his arms around her.

Startled and confused, Laura told Ben she wanted to go home immediately.

"I guess I got a little hysterical because I wasn't sure he'd take me home," Laura said.

Ben drove her home without saying a word, and Laura never heard from him again.

"I felt so humiliated, demeaned," Laura said. "I was angry with Ben for being so abrupt and angry with myself for not knowing how to handle the situation."

And why should she know? The experience was new to her.

Laura's comment, "I felt like a teenager," touched on the truth. The search for a new identity in middle age is, in some ways, a return to the search for identity in adolescence, a time of exploration and discovery that can be beautiful . . . and difficult.

The awkward incident with Ben made Laura wary of going out with a man again for some time.

"I didn't want to be hassled," she said.

She found a temporary, workable substitute by signing up for an exercise class that met three evenings a week at the neighborhood YMCA.

"It gave me something to look forward to," Laura said. "I started losing a little weight and feeling better about myself."

Laura was fighting a tendency of older singles to withdraw from a social life and either molder or complain. Men are even more likely than women to give way to such withdrawal because they fear rejection. Men have their buddies, "the guys," but they're less likely than women to have a confidante with whom they can share personal feelings. One study has shown that only 25 percent of men are willing to talk about personal feelings, compared to 75 percent of women.

Many men who have joined support groups have been pleasantly surprised. When they feel comfortable and relaxed, they can become more open and learn to share their feelings.

"The woman usually stays in the house and keeps up a close relationship with the children," said a divorced man who helped organize a support group. "The man ends up in an apartment or one room feeling completely unwanted. If they only knew!"

The man or woman who chooses to remain in a suburban home may feel isolated in a social life built around the traditional two-parent family. Mark Trowbridge chose to stay on in the two-story Colonial-style house after his wife died of cancer because he didn't want to make any further changes in his life at that time. But, as he pointed out, his artist wife had provided their social contacts and planned their entertaining. Without her, he lost those social contacts.

Single parents with young children often decide to stay in the suburbs because they want to give their children the stability of staying in the same schools, belonging to the same Scout group, taking piano lessons or ballet with their friends. Fine for the children, but the parent may end up feeling like a misfit.

Both men and women turn to work as a substitute for a social life. As a temporary measure, work can provide a healthy outlet. Like many women who find themselves alone, Sara Johnston began to think of her job as a career and to take pleasure in it.

Mark Trowbridge, who had always enjoyed his work, temporarily made work his whole life. Still, he had mentioned wanting a sexual relationship—that "itch."

THE ASSERTIVE WOMAN

Mark's opportunity almost literally dropped out of the sky.

His seatmate on a business trip to Los Angeles was a well-dressed, articulate woman in her late thirties or early forties.

She wore a well-tailored navy-blue suit and crisp white blouse. She looked familiar. On the verge of asking if they had met before, Mark realized she reminded him of actress Jill Clayburgh.

Mark and Janet struck up a conversation shortly after the plane lifted off from LaGuardia Airport. By the time they were sharing cocktails over the Rockies, Mark had told Janet about his wife's death and his current work project. Janet told him she had never married, that she was married to her job as a publicist for one of the motion picture studios. Mark realized he liked Janet. Certainly he felt comfortable talking with her.

"If you don't have plans for this evening, perhaps you'd like to stay at my place," Janet said casually as the plane circled over Los Angeles International Airport. "We can have dinner." Then she added with a smile, "Perhaps you can service me."

Service me. The concept can turn the idea of male conquest 180 degrees. The man becomes the subordinate.

"I'm sorry," Mark said, uneasy with Janet for the first time. "I'm having dinner with some business friends and they may pick me up at the airport."

Mark's business friends did meet him at the airport, and his frank seatmate vanished into the crowds converging toward the baggage claim.

"I'll never know," Mark said. "The thought was tempting because I enjoyed her company. But maybe the role reversal was more than I could handle."

There are many women today, assertive women like Mark's airplane encounter, who refuse to accept the traditional, passive role in a sexual relationship. Mark's reaction of recoil was typical of people whose sexual orientation was formed in an earlier era. Returning to the "outside world" in the 1980s, they tend to misread signals or be put off by another person's direct approach.

OLD FRIENDS IN A NEW LIGHT

"I was brought up with rather strict rules about sex," Sara Johnston said. "I don't want to remarry, but I don't want to live like a nun for the rest of my life. It's difficult. The first thing my doctor asks me when I go for my physical is if I'm having a satisfying sex life. The answer is no."

Sara said two men propositioned her during the first year after her divorce. Both of them were married and were men she had known before her divorce.

She was getting ready for bed one night, watching the eleven o'clock news, when the telephone rang.

"It was my best friend's husband," Sara said. "Jim and I knew the couple for years. He said he was just thinking about me being alone and wondered if there was anything he could do for me."

The full implication of the telephone call didn't really sink in until after Sara had hung up.

"I told him I was managing well and he accepted it," Sara said. "Considering the hour and the tone of his voice, I don't think he was offering to change the washers in my sink or put up the storm windows."

As a result of the incident, she began to feel uneasy about being around the couple or confiding in her friend.

The next proposal was more direct. A dentist who belonged to the same sailing club as Jim invited her to go to New York City for the weekend. She refused, feeling annoyed that the man would make such a presumption.

"He's a colleague of Jim's," Sara said. "I don't know why I'd want to protect Jim's feelings after all he's done to me, but for some reason I never could bring myself to tell Jim what had happened."

Sara was surprised and puzzled by the overtures of her best friend's husband and Jim's colleague, but the fact is involvements between the newly widowed or divorced and trusted old friends are fairly commonplace.

Turning to a known friend is less stressful than looking for a new shoulder to cry on. It's easier to back into such a relationship than to explore new possibilities during the early stages of grief. Remember Elizabeth Taylor's brief marriage to family friend Eddie Fisher after her husband Mike Todd was killed? This kind of involvement is usually based on a deep need to relieve the pain of grief. And as the grief subsides, so does the need.

The penalty can be broken friendships or, in the extreme, broken marriages.

THE DIRECT APPROACH

Singles who advertise for companions in the newspaper or magazines say they like the direct approach.

"You can be completely up front about what you want," said a woman from San Diego. "It cuts out the game playing, the mating ritual."

Until she decided to try a newspaper advertisement, the woman said she had spent some excruciatingly boring evenings with blind dates arranged by friends.

"Why spend a lot of time trying to make conversation with someone when you both know you have nothing whatsoever in common?"

A woman who lives in a rural area of upstate New York said she had no other way of meeting single people. She got seventeen responses to an advertisement she ran in the newspaper of a nearby city.

"You have to use some common sense when you screen them," she cautioned.

She's met some interesting men through her ads, but she said the ads also attract oddballs and kinky propositions. She advised anyone who wants to try a personal advertisement to use a box number, call those that sound interesting, and arrange an initial meeting for coffee or a drink, preferably during the day. She never gives out her telephone number until she's met a man and has decided she would like to see him again.

If the ads in the Strictly Personal column of *New York* magazine are any indication, there are plenty of wealthy, beautiful, successful, classy, warm, and vibrant people out there looking for companions with similar attributes.

Advertisements in local newspapers tend to be less flippant, less tongue in cheek. "I'm lonely," said a sixty-year-old woman who had placed an ad as "a last resort."

She rated her responses only "so-so."

SOCIALIZING PARENTS

Single parents have special problems when it comes to making new social contacts.

"When you've got two young children, a full-time job, and a house to keep up, forget it," Richard Morrison said. "All of a sudden I had to be both parents, and that takes some adjustment."

Richard's first evening out with a woman he had met at a singles club party drew mixed reactions from his children. Four-year-old Jason sat on the bed screaming, begging his father not to leave him. Amanda, his precocious nine-year-old daughter, grilled him with questions about the woman.

"She looks over every woman I meet as a possible new mother," Richard said. "She's quite a matchmaker."

About two years after his wife died, Richard joined the

local chapter of Parents Without Partners, a national group for singles with children. His only regret was that he hadn't joined sooner.

"The people in PWP have become my family," Richard said. "They have a lot of activities the kids and I can enjoy together. It's helped, especially around the holidays."

Being among other single parent families has given his children a sense of security, Richard said. Mandy stopped trying so hard to replace her mother.

As he started meeting more single women, Richard often found it difficult to explain adult relationships to his children. The children were more likely to encourage him to see women he considered only as good friends.

"I've learned to be as up front as possible," Richard said. "I try to remember that their main concern right now is what is going to happen to them."

When Richard meets a woman he's seriously interested in, he invites her home to meet his children.

"That weeds out a few," he said, smiling. "Tell a woman you've got two kids at home and they vanish into the woodwork."

Another single parent we interviewed, a divorced woman, said she finally realized her children were more relaxed if she arranged an informal, brief meeting with a new man in her life. A trip to the ice-cream store or to the public market where she shops on Saturday was easier for everyone than spending a whole evening together the first time. And, she added, "I'd never introduce a date to the children at breakfast."

Divorced or widowed men and women have lost not only the most important person in their life, but many of their friends as well.

The primary goal during these early stages should be making new friends, particularly friends who can empathize. Singles bars, health clubs, or support groups should be regarded simply as informal gathering places where singles meet. When they are used for the express purpose of dating or even meeting a new mate, tension and frustration usually follow.

At the same time, however, the newly single person must retrace the bumpy, uncertain path of adolescence and find a new sexual identity. Debbie's almost casual comment, "Right away I took a guy home and seduced him," was an honest appraisal of her need to explore, to prove she was still sexually appealing. Judy kept kidding herself and looking for "the real thing."

Sexual identity occurs on three levels—for "myself," for the temporary relationship, and finally, for an intimate, permanent relationship. Debbie and Judy were still a long way from being ready for real intimacy.

Older singles usually find it difficult to experiment sexually, particularly if they were married for a long time. Despite his "itch," Mark didn't go to bed with the first woman who showed an interest in him. Sara wasn't tempted by overtures from her best friend's husband and her ex-husband's business associate. Laura refused to date after the first pass in the front seat of a car.

Yet they were beginning to make progress in their own ways.

Mark had met Jennifer and a circle of new friends in his photography class. Laura was going out to an exercise class three evenings a week and beginning to feel better about herself. Sara was beginning to think of her part-time job in terms of an interesting career. Richard, having overcome his negative impressions of support groups, was beginning to socialize with other single parents and their children.

All were taking small but important steps toward recovery.

6: LIFE CHANGES

A divorced career woman said she choked up one day in the supermarket.

"The woman ahead of me was unloading her shopping cart with meat and vegetables, gallon jugs of milk, a big bag of gingersnaps," the woman recalled. "I had seven Lean Cuisines, two bottles of tonic water, and a jar of macadamia nuts. I looked at her stuff and then at mine. I didn't like what it said about my life."

Another woman we interviewed made the bemused observation, "I couldn't even generate trash after my husband left. We used to fill four barrels a week. I'm thinking about borrowing a couple of bags from the neighbors."

The dinner hour was difficult for a recently divorced man.

"My wife and I used to have a drink and talk while we fixed dinner together, but now I eat whatever happens to be handy." He added with amusement, "Then I get up and do the dish."

The pattern of daily life changes overnight for the widowed and divorced. Shared responsibilities have to be rethought. If she cooked, who will do the cooking now that he is gone?

If he washed the dog, who will wash the dog now that he is gone? One man gave his wife a Johnny Mop as a farewell present. His weekly chore had been cleaning the bathrooms.

Professionals advise the divorced and widowed to postpone making any further changes in their lives at this point. The body can handle only so much change at one time.

In some cases, changes have to be made for practical reasons such as a financial crisis or poor health. But often a person going through a painful transition feels compelled to make changes that aren't really necessary. Judy Carpenter moved to New York City to get a fresh start, but that move required still further adjustments. Feeling angry and upset, Sara Johnston threw her wedding dress and some mementos from her honeymoon into the trash after her husband left her. Later, in a more rational frame of mind, she regretted destroying some things her children might have wanted.

It takes some quiet reflection, preferably with the understanding help of a close friend or family member, to decide what must be done immediately and what changes can be postponed for a period of time, or indefinitely.

MONEY, THE NUMBER-ONE PROBLEM

Money is the biggest problem most people face after a divorce or the death of their mate, and women tend to be the most vulnerable. One study shows that a man's spendable income goes up 42 percent following a divorce, while a woman's income plummets by 60 percent. The primary reason is that men become single, while women often become single parents.

Men who pay large sums for child support, alimony, or both can argue that these figures don't tell the whole story.

"I'm driving a 1972 Chevy so I can support the world's oldest college sophomore," said a disgruntled thirty-seven-year-old executive. "She's driving the BMW."

The court ordered him to pay $600 a month in child support, his children's medical and dental expenses, and his wife's expenses for three years until she obtained her college degree. The divorce was bitter, and the man resented the financial drain even for a specified period of time.

Sara Johnston was more fortunate. Her ex-husband, Jim, eager to get the divorce, accepted the court-ordered division of property and agreed to pay Sara's expenses for graduate school. Despite the generous settlement, Sara knew that she would eventually have to support herself. For women like Sara who gave up careers to raise a family, the thought of earning a living after a lapse of many years can be frightening. For women who have never worked, the fear can be mind boggling.

Why is money such a key issue? Not, as one might think, for financial security, but because money is equated with power. The executive who is ordered to pay large child support payments or alimony, the widow who must suddenly get by on Social Security benefits, both translate their new situations into a loss of control over their lives.

The relationship between behavior and human needs was explored by behavioral scientist Abraham Maslow when he developed the Maslow Need Hierarchy of five levels. The basic level represents physiological and survival goals, including food, shelter, clothing, sex, and other essentials. The second level consists of safety needs, represented by such factors as an adequate salary and insurance policies.

Only after most of these lower-level needs have been met can the individual begin to develop interpersonal relationships and move into the third stage of "belongingness." Third-level needs concern friendships, family ties, and group membership. Once the individual feels secure in "belonging," he or she begins to seek special status within the group and attempts to achieve "ego-status" needs on the fourth level of the hierarchy and, finally, the highest level of self-actualization and personal growth.

Divorce or the death of one's mate frequently disrupts the process, forcing a person who has been functioning on the upper levels to regress and become concerned again about fulfilling basic needs. When this happens, behavior changes. Sara Johnston, Laura Cunningham, and Richard Morrison were now motivated by survival needs.

One woman described the change in her financial situation after her divorce this way:

"We had plenty of money for the two of us," she said. "Now neither of us has enough."

LOOKING FOR ALTERNATIVES

Although Sara Johnston had a modest income from her part-time job, the house, a cash settlement from the divorce, and a maintenance allowance from Jim for two years, she still had financial problems.

"I've got the house, and it's probably worth about a hundred and fifty thousand dollars right now, but you can't take a house to the supermarket," Sara pointed out. "In fact, the house is a burden financially. The upkeep is costing almost as much as I make at the hospital."

Sara's salary had been the couple's supplemental income before her divorce. She had felt free to spend the money she made on designer clothes, a special vacation, or something extra for the house. After the divorce, she had to spend her income on essentials and found it didn't go far.

"I want to stay in the house until I figure out what to do," Sara said. "I know I should be going back to school for graduate work because that was in the agreement. I can't even handle that right now."

It was Sara's daughter who first suggested she should consider sharing the house with another single woman.

"A lot of my friends are house sharing because they can't afford to buy a house on their own," Sara's daughter told her.

"Besides, I'd feel better if you had someone living here with you. New London isn't New York City, but I still worry about you living alone."

At first, Sara rejected the idea. She didn't like the thought of having a stranger around all the time. What if the person turned out to be sloppy or inconsiderate? She could get stuck in a situation, or at least find it hard to get out of.

But the idea had been planted. A few months later, Sara read a notice on the bulletin board in her office. A woman who had been hired recently was looking for an apartment near the hospital.

"Have you found a place to live?" Sara asked her the following day, almost hoping she had.

Betsy Riechert was an outgoing, stocky woman with an Afro hairdo who had been hired to run the hospital's new computer system. No, she hadn't found a place to live.

Sara invited Betsy over for dinner and showed her around the house, a one-hundred-year-old saltbox on a quiet street.

"I love the house, but I'm not sure I could afford my share of the expenses," Betsy said at the end of the evening. "Let's think about it."

In the exchange of information over dinner, Betsy had told Sara she was forty-one and had been divorced for almost ten years. She had a son in college who usually spent Thanksgiving or Christmas with her, dividing the two holidays between Betsy and his father. Betsy said she and her former husband had managed to stay on good terms.

Sara liked Betsy's friendly, open manner. She was aware of the contrast to her own anxious, uptight feelings.

Weeks passed. Sara and Betsy had lunch together several times, but the subject of sharing the house never came up. Sara had almost put it out of her mind.

"Hey, let's try it," Betsy said one day. "I love the old inn, but it isn't convenient and it's getting expensive."

Sara suggested moving her personal belongings out of the

family room to give Betsy a private living room as well as the largest guest room upstairs. They would each have a private bath but would have to share the kitchen and dining room.

After talking it over, they agreed to share the cost of groceries and cooking.

"I had a roommate in college who put her initials on her eggs," Betsy said. "I'd like to be looser about it than that."

Betsy moved in on a Saturday, showing up early in the morning in blue jeans and an oversized sweatshirt. If she noticed Sara's red-rimmed eyes and sober expression, she didn't mention it.

Clearing her personal items out of the den had, unexpectedly, opened a lot of Sara's wounds. The den was filled with mementos of family trips and vacations, with the photograph albums Sara had filled from the time the children were babies until they'd gone away to college. As Sara cleaned out the closet, a Mexican sombrero fell off the top shelf. Jim had bought it in Mexico City and, in a frivolous mood, had put it on that night in their room. Slightly drunk on margaritas, they had made love in the big carved bed. Sara remembered the whirring of the ceiling fan above them and the warm air against her skin as she'd lain back, relaxed, against the pillows.

"Damn you, Jim," Sara said aloud. "How could you throw it all away?"

Would she always feel this way? Was life worth living with nothing but painful memories?

Betsy's arrival had pulled Sara abruptly back to the present, reminding her of all they had to do. Sara and Betsy worked hard all day, carrying heavy boxes from Betsy's car and moving furniture. By the time Betsy was finally settled in, Sara was exhausted, dirty, and sweaty.

"Let's forget cooking and order a pizza," Betsy suggested when they finally collapsed.

Sara would eat a lot more pizza than she cared to during Betsy's stay in her house. And she would do more than her share of the cooking and cleaning. But Betsy's cheerful presence would give Sara reassurance, a kind of ballast for her own shaky existence.

Sharing her house and the expenses filled one of Sara's most important needs—the need to postpone. She wasn't emotionally prepared to make a major adjustment in her life by giving up her job and entering graduate school. In fact, her job provided the one stabilizing influence in her life at that point.

Betsy's friendship was just what Sara needed to start thinking ahead. Betsy didn't know Jim or Sara's old friends, so instead of dwelling at length on the past, the two of them could talk about their jobs and their plans.

Further, Betsy's cheerful, relaxed attitude gave Sara "reassurance," a key point. The divorced and widowed look for anchors.

Too often, the handiest anchors are remnants from the past. One of the widows we interviewed continued to attend the annual parties at a company where her husband had worked for thirty years. Instead of feeling reassured by longtime acquaintances, the woman found the parties to be painful reminders that she no longer "belonged." After discussing her feelings with a therapist, she wisely stopped going. She had grabbed for the wrong anchor.

A WIFE'S WORTH

Money was the last thing on Richard Morrison's mind when his young wife died suddenly of a heart attack. Within a few months, however, he was dipping into their savings to pay household expenses.

"Her insurance policy barely covered the cost of the funeral," Richard said. "I just can't seem to get a handle on where the money's going."

A novice in the supermarket, Richard admitted he spent more money on groceries than Peggy had. When he was too tired to cook, he took the children out for dinner. The cost of Jason's day care and baby-sitters when Richard couldn't get out of an evening appointment added up. The weekly cleaning woman and having to send his shirts to the laundry took another bite. Richard was paying for a lot of services his wife had performed.

At the same time, his insurance sales commissions began to drop.

"I used to make a lot of my sales in the evening," Richard said. "Being with the kids has priority now."

Although his supervisor remained understanding, Richard was beginning to sense some resentment from the other agents who had to take over for him. He worried about what would happen if he lost his job.

Richard was also increasingly worried about his son. Jason was shy and withdrawn at the day care center, the teacher told him. And despite Richard's efforts to be Superdad, Jason often cried himself to sleep at night.

The emotional and physical drain took its toll. After a particularly difficult week when everything seemed to be falling apart at home and at work, Richard collapsed at the office. He was admitted to the hospital, where the doctors diagnosed extreme exhaustion. Family counselors call it "role overload," a common ailment of single parents.

"That's when I had to admit I needed help," Richard said. "Up to that time, I suppose I was trying to prove something—that I could handle it."

Richard called his mother and asked her to come and stay with the children until he got out of the hospital.

By the time he was released, he had worked out a plan and

presented it to the neighbor next door. Would she be willing to take care of Jason during the day if they could work out a suitable fee? Reluctant to charge him at first, she finally agreed. Jason was happier in familiar surroundings. The neighbor didn't charge as much as the day care center had cost, and she liked the idea of making some extra money without leaving her home.

A woman Richard had met at Parents Without Partners who had a daughter Mandy's age had told him she'd be glad to take Mandy shopping for school clothes. Richard had gratefully accepted the offer. The first outing went so well she started picking Mandy up almost every Saturday.

"She offered to talk to Mandy about the facts of life," Richard said. "I had tried to broach the subject, but it was awkward for both of us."

The most unexpected source of help turned out to be the children themselves. Richard went over his budget and decided they could do without the cleaning woman. He made out a list of chores and divided it up among the three of them.

"They complain," Richard said with a slight smile, "but I think secretly they're proud of themselves."

Finally, Richard managed to change his attitude, to set more realistic standards.

"If they miss a little dust or the bed isn't made exactly right, I don't let it bother me. I worried about everything at first. Now I know somehow things do work out."

As Richard discovered, housekeeping changes when one partner is gone.

"Suddenly, you're doing your own bathrooms," he said. "You don't find clean shirts and underwear in the dresser drawers anymore."

The woman who has been the primary housekeeper suddenly asks herself, "For what?" If her husband has taken care of the outside chores, she'll have to figure out how to keep the yardwork up and the cars running.

Richard failed miserably when he tried to follow the old patterns established when Peggy was alive. Finally, he took an important step. He came up with a plan and a method to implement his plan. Once Richard recognized there aren't any rewards for physical endurance, he was able to ask for help and change his priorities.

LAURA GETS ORGANIZED

For more than two years after her husband died suddenly of a heart attack, Laura Cunningham simply lowered her standard of living and "made do." She didn't buy any new clothes. She didn't fix up the house. If an appliance broke, she tried to get along without it.

"I didn't even balance the checkbook," Laura said. "Nothing seemed to matter to me anymore."

David had put his life insurance into a trust fund that provided Laura with a modest monthly income. She received quarterly dividends from the stock David had accumulated in a stock purchase plan with his company. The income paid for groceries, and with a little juggling and help from the dividends, Laura could keep up with the utility bills and Marcie's school expenses. Marcie earned spending money by babysitting in the neighborhood.

Laura might have continued to drift along in this way if she hadn't received a notice from the bank that her checking account was overdrawn.

"Dammit, I've got to get organized," Laura said to herself, surveying the piles of unpaid bills, receipts, and unopened bank statements she had tossed carelessly into the desk drawers.

Laura cleaned and sorted through papers all afternoon. She examined her canceled checks against the bank statements and finally found the error. The bank had continued to make monthly deductions for a charity David had supported.

"Charity," she said softly to herself. "Right now, charity begins at home."

The clean desk and balanced checkbook made Laura feel good. She was still sitting there when Marcie got home from school.

"I've just been thinking, maybe I ought to get a job," Laura said. "We're just barely getting by."

"A job," Marcie echoed, frowning slightly. "What kind of a job?"

Laura had to think about that. She had worked as a secretary before she and David were married and until their first child was born. She considered brushing up on her typing and shorthand but decided she was too old to compete with younger people going into the field. She'd feel lost in a new, computerized office, she was quite certain.

Laura started reading the newspaper employment ads every morning over a second cup of coffee. Accountant . . . with experience. Advertising director . . . with experience. Auto mechanic . . . with experience. Even belly dancers and bus drivers needed experience.

Laura had already considered selling the house and had rejected the idea. Although the house was bigger than she needed and she couldn't afford to keep it up properly, the old place and its familiar neighborhood gave her a feeling of security.

"The man at the gas station knows me and I can trust him to keep my car going. It's good to see familiar faces on the street and to shop in stores where I'm known. I'd lose that even if we moved across town."

After job hunting for about three months, Laura finally got an offer as a housewares clerk in a department store.

"I sort of went in there with an I-don't-suppose-you-want-to-hire-me attitude," Laura said later. "I was pretty tense until I realized I could handle the work as well as anyone."

Laura did her job not only as well as, but better than, most of the clerks in her department. She was patient in her dealings with customers and didn't complain if she was asked to work overtime or take on extra responsibility.

"It's not the greatest job, but it gives me a reason to get up in the morning. Besides, I get a discount at the store. Marcie and I both are getting new clothes, and I'm beginning to fix up the house."

Like most older women who go back to work after raising a family, Laura sold herself short. She didn't realize that running a house and raising children had given her experience many employers look for. She had learned how to organize, set priorities, and manage time. She understood the value of working hard to finish a job and the importance of being consistent.

It didn't occur to Laura that her volunteer work had given her some valuable experience. She had helped on fund-raising drives, made presentations before groups, and served as chairman for a major fashion show. By making up a "skills resume" rather than a work resume, Laura could have shown she was qualified for a variety of jobs.

A number of agencies have been set up to help women and older workers find employment. The Displaced Homemakers Network, based in Washington, D.C., works through community colleges, YMCAs, and other local agencies. GROW (Gaining Resources for Older Workers) offers counseling, training, and job placement for unemployed men and women who are forty-five and over. The service is free. Women's Career Centers provide counseling and assistance on changing or starting a new career.

By contacting one of these agencies, Laura could have gotten help in identifying her abilities and writing up a resume, which would have showed her how these skills could be transferred to the job market. Although she ended up satisfied with her clerking job, she might have found a more interesting and better-paying job.

SAYING GOOD-BYE

Mark Trowbridge lived in his four-bedroom house in a suburb of Dallas for two years after his wife died of cancer.

"Your body can only take so many changes at one time," Mark said. "Anyone who won't accept that fact is just fooling himself."

Mark could afford his luxurious home. Connie's death had had an emotional impact on his life but hadn't affected him financially. An artist, Connie had sold an occasional painting for what she had laughingly called her "egg money"—a reference to the days when farmers' wives sold eggs to earn extra spending money.

"She had a small, ten-thousand-dollar life insurance policy," Mark said. "I divided that up among the three children as a kind of personal bequest from their mother."

Mark knew he didn't want to keep up the family house alone indefinitely, so he set a time frame.

"I decided to give myself two years before making any decisions on where I wanted to live or what to do about the furniture and personal things. I talked this over with the children. They live in other parts of the country, and I wanted them to come to Dallas when the time came so that we could go through everything together."

For Mark and his children, sorting through all the personal things the family had accumulated over the years and deciding what to do about the furniture was an important step in accepting their loss.

The children spent a week in Dallas. They dragged out the

skis and remembered vacations in Aspen and Austria. They opened trunks and cried over old letters. They discovered all their school report cards carefully preserved. They piled rusty bicycles and broken sleds by the curb. The children each picked certain things to keep that had special meaning. The week brought them closer together. As they put old memories to rest, they completed the mourning process. When the children left, Mark started looking at apartments.

"It's adequate," Mark said with a sweeping gesture around the duplex apartment he chose on the outskirts of the city, about a fifteen-minute drive from his office.

Mark had sorted through all the books in the house and kept his favorites. These and a new hi-fi system filled one wall of his living room. He had sold most of the furniture except for a favorite cherry Windsor desk in his bedroom. In contrast with the traditional furniture he and his wife had chosen for the house, the apartment was furnished in modern, functional pieces. A deep, comfortable sofa and a pair of chairs were upholstered in brown tweed. The pecan tables were sturdily built in smooth, uncluttered lines. The rooms were immaculate.

"It's adequate," Mark said again. "I spend so much time traveling and so many evenings with clients, it's a treat to have an evening here alone just listening to music."

Mark's decision to postpone the sale of the house and to include his children when the time came showed wisdom and sensitivity. Then, after two years, he could face the task of sorting out family belongings and make rational decisions about what he wanted to keep. Asking the children to participate was a way of recognizing that this was their loss, too. The week they spent together and the recollection of family memories was a kind of farewell ritual that enabled them to finally resolve their grief.

At some point, every person who is left alone must decide what to do about the house and their loved one's personal belongings. Usually the first instinct is to keep the house because it represents security. Only after they've begun to regain control in other areas of their life are they ready to think about moving. It takes most people a year or two before they can comfortably move into new surroundings. At that point, they can say with a degree of dispassion, "That was my marriage residence."

The lost mate's personal belongings can be comforting to the widowed in the early stages of grief. Laura Cunningham felt comforted when she saw David's clothes in the closet and sat in his favorite easy chair. Comedian George Burns said he couldn't sleep for weeks after his wife, Gracie, died, until finally he got into her bed, where he slept peacefully.

The reaction is often just the opposite in the case of divorce. Sara Johnston was upset when she came across a Mexican sombrero that brought back bittersweet memories. An item of clothing Jim had left behind or a smiling family photograph could reopen painful wounds.

"Pack all these things into boxes as soon as one partner moves out and put them in some out-of-the way corner," advises Dr. Dennis Boike.

Most people said they knew instinctively when the time came to part with these things.

"David's old blue sweater was still hanging on the porch where he always put it when he came in from gardening," Laura Cunningham said. "I didn't want it moved. Almost a year later, and I'm not sure why I chose that particular day to do it, I folded it up and put it away. Right after that, I called the Salvation Army and donated his clothing. I felt good that someone would get some use out of it."

After his wife, Peggy, died suddenly, Richard Morrison asked Mrs. Parker, Peggy's mother, to take Peggy's clothes and decide what to do with them. He kept the purse Peggy had left on the bedroom dresser but couldn't bring himself to open it. It seemed like an invasion of her privacy. He put the purse on a shelf in the bedroom closet and left it there for a year or two.

One evening he took it off the shelf and, sitting on the bed, started to go through it. A half-used lipstick. A grocery list. A worn billfold. Richard took out the money and Peggy's Social Security card, dropping the rest into the wastebasket.

"That night I remembered Peggy's habit of carrying mad money," Richard said. "I found the billfold in the trash and, sure enough, there was a twenty-dollar bill in the secret compartment. I just sat there for a while, thinking about her. Another time, I don't think I could have handled it."

WHEN THERE ARE FEW RESOURCES

If Mark Trowbridge could be said to represent a person in charge of his crisis, Frank Gardener would have to represent the opposite. When Frank's wife, Jill, left him to marry his best friend, Frank fell into limbo.

Frank didn't have Mark's emotional or financial stability. The death of his mother when he was fifteen had been a lethal blow, but he had tried to emulate his dispassionate father and "be a man."

Having learned in his youth to withdraw and deny pain, Frank had appeared almost numb through the divorce proceedings. When the divorce was final, Frank went back to the house for the last time to pack his clothes and personal belongings.

After he'd folded the last load of clothes from the dryer and packed them into the open suitcases on the bed, he looked around the bedroom. A smiling photograph of Jill on the dresser seemed to taunt him, and he turned away.

He walked slowly through the house, remembering their first night there. They had sat cross-legged on the floor eating hamburgers, French fries, and milk shakes from a fast-food restaurant down the road while waiting for the overdue moving van to arrive.

"Our first real home," Jill had sighed, and Frank had thought she looked beautiful despite the smudges of dirt on her face.

Had he ever told Jill how much having a real home had meant to him? From the time his mother had died, Frank had been more or less on his own. He had stayed in the house with his father and two older brothers, but the house had never felt like a home again; his mother was no longer there when he got home from school, no hugs, no aroma of dinner cooking in the kitchen, no admonitions when he sneaked out to play basketball without doing his homework.

Frank's two brothers started getting into trouble, first at school and then with the law. He could remember his father yelling and beating them. Frank had been determined to get out and finally had managed to do so, paying his way by taking any odd job he could find.

Had he ever told Jill just how much her warmth and kindness had meant to him? From almost the first time Jill had waited on him in the bookstore of the community college he was attending, Frank had looked for any excuse to stop by and talk to her. Sometimes he would hang around until she was off work, and they would walk together across campus. When he had money, he would ask her to go out to a movie or to a tavern near the campus. Frank had wanted to ask her to marry him, but in the end it was Jill who'd proposed.

"We can make it," she'd said one evening when they had been talking about the future. "I'll stop working part-time and get a full-time job."

And they had made it, Frank thought. First the house, then the babies. Maybe he'd never be able to put it into words, but this house and having a family had meant a lot to him. Frank shook his head.

He made a last check of the closets and found his old ski jacket. Tossing it on the bed, he snapped the suitcases shut.

As he loaded the boxes and suitcases into the station wagon, Frank noticed some curious children standing near the driveway watching him.

"Cheers," he said with a little salute.

As he climbed into the driver's seat, Frank remembered he had left his fishing gear and some tools in the basement. He hesitated. Then he shrugged and started the car.

Frank drove in a daze. He was tired, and when he saw the lights of a liquor store, he stopped and bought a bottle of Wild Turkey. Farther down the road, he saw the flashing lights of a motel and pulled over.

The motel room seemed bleak and lonely. Frank filled a glass from the bathroom with whiskey and took a long drink. He lay back on the bed and switched on the music.

Frank stared at the ceiling. He felt better. He had another drink, and another. Sometime later, after the bottle was empty, Frank was dimly aware of Willie Nelson's voice on the radio.

"Maybe I never told you half as much as I should have. But you were always on my mind. You were always on my mind."

Frank turned his face toward the wall. Much later, he was awakened by an impatient pounding on his door. It was the maid, but before he could pull himself up, she moved on and started knocking on the next door. And then Frank realized, the pounding was in his head.

He rented the first apartment he found that was in his price range, an efficiency on the second floor of an old house with a fold-out couch in the living room and a small Pullman-type kitchen.

"I'm on the road so much, I just need a place to hang my hat," Frank told the talkative landlady, who was showing him the nice view of the garden and pointing out how convenient the apartment was to the shopping area.

About six months later Frank's car broke down, and the mechanic told him it needed major repairs. With the car in the garage, Frank didn't have a way to pick up the children that weekend. Already at odds with Jill over his delinquent child support payments, Frank couldn't bring himself to call her and explain.

"Now she's accusing me of not wanting to see the kids," Frank said. "She's trying to turn them against me."

Normally thin, Frank had lost weight, and his eyes looked sunken, shadowed.

"The doctor says I've got hypoglycemia," he said. "Too much sugar."

The partner who stays in the home has significant adjustments to make, but consider the leaver—the partner who moves out.

When moving out actually means moving in with an attractive third party, the leaver probably won't miss the old routine, at least not for a while. If Sara Johnston's husband, Jim, felt a twinge about leaving the gracious saltbox-style house where he had lived with Sara for so many years, he had a new relationship to distract him.

But for Frank, moving out of the house and the familiar neighborhood held no such promises.

In a more rational state of mind, Frank could have taken some steps to make his life more bearable and to salvage his relationship with his children. He could have explained his financial problems to Jill and worked out a plan to make up the child support payments. If she'd refused to cooperate, he could have gone to court for a change in his visitation rights. He could have taken more interest in looking for an apartment with room enough for the children to visit him. He could have done these things, but only in a more rational state of mind.

Typically, Frank took the path of least resistance. When he was fifteen, his father had admonished him to be a man, and Frank was still biting the bullet.

Frank's personality may have made the adjustment particularly difficult for him, but others we interviewed described similar feelings of being set adrift when they moved out of their house and familiar surroundings.

"I asked my secretary to go out and buy everything I needed to outfit the apartment," said a divorced professional man. "Then I asked her to lay out my clothes for the week."

The months following the death of a spouse or a divorce can also be a time when everything seems to "go wrong." Appliances break down. Accidents happen. Health problems seem to occur more frequently.

"You expect bad days," Frank said later. "That was a bad year."

TWO HOMES

As single parents struggle with the changes in their daily lives, their children are forced to make some significant adjustments, too.

Kristen Carpenter came to enjoy the advantages of spending her winters in New York City and her summers in Boulder, Colorado. The adjustment to New York took some time, she said.

"I hated the city at first. They had a lot of cliques at the school, and I felt like they all looked down on me because of the way I dressed. They thought I was a hick. I met this one girl who seemed real friendly. Right away she asked me if I got high. When I said I didn't, she just laughed and didn't speak to me after that."

By the second year, Kristen had met a group of young people she liked. She had dreaded telling them she'd be going out west in the spring, but they actually seemed to envy her.

"I think the hardest part is adjusting to different house rules," Kristen said. "Mom expects me to share the housework, and she's really strict about knowing where I am all the time. With Dad I can get by with anything. He's a lot more relaxed." Then she laughed and added, "He's a little uptight when I want to go out with a boy. Not too relaxed about that!"

Packing and leaving was usually a wrench, Kristen said.

"There's always something coming up that I really want to go to. It seems like wherever I am, I don't want to leave. I'm homesick for a while, always on the telephone."

Kristen was angry with her parents at first, but finally she accepted the divorce. She said her parents helped.

"They get along pretty well. I've heard some horror stories from other kids, so I guess I'm lucky."

The divorce changed her attitude about marriage. When she was younger, she would go to a family wedding and daydream about being a bride. Romantic ideas.

"I don't know if I'll get married," she said thoughtfully. "If I do, I'll make sure we stay together."

Children adjust more easily to change if they're told the facts without being overwhelmed. And following a divorce, they need quality time with and access to each parent. Finally, children can make the transition more easily if the parents transcend personal conflicts to work in relative harmony toward good parenting.

Joint custody would appear to be the best answer. Ideally, the parents would continue to share responsibility for their children just as they did when they were married. The potential of joint custody looks so promising that some states now require it be offered as one of the options for all divorcing parents.

The reality is not as promising, however. "Joint custody is

a great idea, but not for everyone," said family therapist Susan Horwitz. "The parents' goals and values must be congruent, and each must be able to support the other in some way. Often divorcing couples cannot get beyond their own resentment and anger. They allow these feelings to seep into their parenting relationship. This can be disastrous for kids."

Joint custody was one of the topics considered at a conference on the family sponsored by the National Institutes of Health in Washington, D.C.

"Joint custody is too complex to mandate," said Professor Thomas Langner of Columbia University, one of seven professionals who participated. "There is often a lot of conflict, or one parent may be abusive. The fact is, something less than half of divorced fathers have any contact with their children after the first year, a discouraging statistic."

Even when children do have contact with both parents, relationships change. Some fathers become "Disneyland dads" or "weekend uncles." They feel as if they have to entertain their children during their visitation time.

"I resented my husband a lot in the beginning because he always did special things with the kids," one divorced woman said. "I had to handle the nitty-gritty—the discipline problems, taking care of them when they were sick. Why *wouldn't* they think he was something special?"

Considering the geographical distance between them and the differences in their values, Judy and Stephen Carpenter handled the joint custody arrangement fairly well. Kristen spent enough time with each of them to fall into a relaxed family routine. Neither Judy nor Stephen had to take on the role of outsider or special visitor. Kristen had the stability of staying in the same place during the school year and, at the same time, staying in touch with old friends in Boulder. Both Judy and Stephen proved by their actions that they were interested in their daughter's welfare.

Divorce or the death of a parent forces children to make some major adjustments in the way they live. They need all the stability their parents can muster.

As Dr. Boike puts it, "Kids need a place to barnacle."

"Postpone" is the watchword for the newly widowed and divorced.

Postpone decisions. Postpone further changes. Enough major changes are already taking place. The stories above illustrate changes in (1) attitudes about money, (2) friendships, (3) attitudes toward jobs and careers, (4) housekeeping, (5) relationships with children, (6) self-esteem, (7) sex life, and (8) communication with others.

Mark's two-year plan enabled him to adjust to many of these changes before he gave up the family home and moved into an apartment.

Sara couldn't afford to wait two years before making a decision. Sharing her house and living expenses with another single woman provided a logical solution to her financial problems.

Sometimes asking for help is the only realistic way to take up the slack when one person is trying to be two parents. Richard found it difficult to admit he couldn't "handle it." When he finally collapsed, he got the help he needed from his family, a neighbor, a friend, and, surprisingly, his children.

A job turned out to be a positive step for Laura, who had been barely getting by and making do. With more initiative and a healthier self-esteem, Laura could probably have gotten a better job, but at least she was heading in the right direction.

Frank's story illustrates what can happen when changes occur too rapidly too soon. Still in the early stages of grief, he couldn't quite connect with reality. Eventually he would find an anchor and begin to rebuild his life.

7: THE EMOTIONAL RECOVERY

Laura Cunningham looked up from her book as Marcie came down the stairs dressed in yellow ski pants and a warm white sweater.

"I can skip this ski trip and we can do something to celebrate your birthday this evening," Marcie said. "It doesn't seem right for you to be by yourself." Marcie's offer was made in the belated realization that the weekend ski trip with her club at school coincided with her mother's birthday.

Laura shook her head. "I'll finish my book," she said, keeping her tone as casual as possible. The fact was, she didn't feel like celebrating. "Besides, I didn't get a letter from Nancy today, so I'm sure she'll be calling this evening."

Her friend Nancy always remembered Laura's birthday with a long, newsy letter, a funny card, or a gag present. Nancy had sent a lily and a sympathy card on Laura's fiftieth.

"If you're sure," Marcie said, grabbing her coat and running to answer the doorbell. "I'll see you tomorrow afternoon."

Marcie had put a birthday card and a small bottle of Laura's favorite perfume on her breakfast plate that morning. Laura had almost forgotten the custom she had started when the children were young—putting a card or small gift on their breakfast plate on special holidays and birthdays. The small gesture had rekindled pleasant memories, which in turn reminded her that those days were over.

Holidays, birthdays, their wedding anniversary, the anniversary of David's death—all had been difficult days for Laura. But somehow she had survived the cycle two times. Two years. She felt stronger, less vulnerable. She was finally resuming her life, feeling more like a participant again instead of a helpless bystander. Why was she depressed now?

Laura tried to concentrate on her book. It was a new historical novel, and she had been looking forward to escaping into a romantic adventure story. She read a paragraph over three times before she finally put it down.

Sighing, she went out to the kitchen and poured a glass of milk. She decided not to bother fixing lunch.

David had always taken her out to dinner on her birthday. Laura remembered the time he'd ordered a miniature birthday cake with one sparkling candle and the waiters had gathered around the table to sing "Happy Birthday."

"David, don't ever do this again," she had said, embarrassed, her face flushing.

And he never had. She had negated his thoughtfulness. Why hadn't she thanked him? Guilt nagged at her.

Laura sat at the kitchen table, aware of the stillness. She tried to remember other specific instances that might be responsible for her vague feelings of guilt and remorse. Her thoughts filtered through disconnected images, unable to focus.

Hours passed. It was almost midnight before Laura accepted the fact that Nancy wasn't going to call. She went upstairs and stretched out across the bed, not bothering to undress. She listened to the wind creak through the rafters of the old house. Why had everyone, even her best friend, abandoned her?

• • •

Laura's erratic feelings confused her. She had always considered herself a fairly stable, happy person before David died, and recently she had begun to regain a sense of contentment. Then, out of the blue, some relatively insignificant event—a forgotten birthday—had shattered her.

Laura would have been comforted, better able to deal with this stage of her grief, if she had understood and accepted her negative feelings as a valid part of the complex process of mourning.

People are "entitled" to feel what they feel, writes Ann S. Kliman in *Crisis*.

Guilt, remorse, abandonment, the worst must be felt. In the first go-through after a significant loss, one is more apt to feel sadness, certainly free of any blame for the event. But in the second go-through, people can beat on themselves, sometimes mercilessly.

The cycles recur just as the very rhythm of life is one of recurring progression and regression. We hear it every day. "I was just getting squared away and . . ." Something happens.

"We just got the last child through college and . . . I got this pain in my chest."

"I was just getting my weight down and . . . the party season is starting."

"We just got the bills paid and . . . the washing machine broke."

Laura was just beginning to feel better and . . . unexpected depression hit.

Most of us manage life's inevitable cycle of broken washing machines fairly well. We know what to do about such events. It's more difficult to cope with normal wear and tear on the psyche. We want life to make sense. When it doesn't, we're confused.

Consciously, settled with a good book to read, Laura didn't

mind spending her birthday alone. She anticipated her friend Nancy's call. But Laura couldn't afford the tension. Like a drowning person, she grabbed for a log to give her some relief and it sank. The call didn't come.

David Curtiss, a fifty-three-year-old research chemist, described a similar occurrence about eight months after his wife died suddenly of a stroke. She had become ill one evening in their home and died two days later in the hospital. For several weeks, David would wake up with a start about four A.M., his pulse racing. Although a comfortable driver for many years, he suddenly couldn't drive the car. He couldn't concentrate. David accepted these symptoms of acute stress as a natural reaction to his wife's death, and they subsided gradually over a period of several weeks.

About eight months later, David visited a friend who was recuperating from minor surgery in the same hospital where his wife had died.

"The visit was upbeat in every way," David recalled. "My friend looked great, and he was talking about going back to work right away. I came away feeling really good about it."

The next morning, David woke up with a start about four A.M. The stress symptoms had returned. "That's when I had to accept the power of the subconscious," said David.

Despite his severe, debilitating symptoms, it never occurred to David to get professional help, to seek out a support group, or even to discuss his feelings with a close, understanding friend.

"I assumed," he said with a sigh, "that's just how it is."

Unfortunately, all too many still share David's belief, suffering silently, often needlessly, through the erratic stages of grief. Yet more and more are also finding they can be helped by understanding the grief process and what can be done to ease the pain.

FEELING STUCK

There are no simple how-to's for emotional recovery from the loss of a mate. A lot of attention has been focused on how to rekindle a social life, adjust to living alone, and learn to love again. Join a club. Get your hair styled. Buy a dog and take it for outings. Indeed, divorce is sometimes portrayed as a "second chance" and life alone as a "new beginning." Articles and books in this positive, upbeat vein can be a disservice to the person who's still suffering.

As one woman put it, "I read in magazines that I should get out and join a club. I'm still working on getting dressed in the morning."

The woman was stuck, for the time being "on hold" emotionally. Her reading friends, even the woman herself, failed to recognize that she was temporarily immobilized and that this is a common reaction to acute stress. Unable to take action on her own, the woman needed help. A skilled therapist or separation adjustment group could have provided that help.

FIRST STEPS

Dr. J. William Worden, a psychotherapist and researcher in the field of terminal illness and suicide, defines the four "tasks" of mourning. First, a person must accept the reality of the loss. Second, one must experience the pain of grief. Third, the person must adjust to the environment in which the loved one is missing. And fourth, one must withdraw emotional energy and reinvest in another relationship.

Incompleted grief work can impair growth and development, Worden notes in *Grief Counseling and Grief Therapy,* a handbook for the mental health practitioner. Unresolved grief can lead to mental health problems and delayed grief reactions.

Accepting the loss of a loved one through death or divorce

can be accomplished by "saying good-bye" when the person is ready to take this step—that is, to take leave of the other as someone irrevocably gone.

One man showed remarkable insight in accepting the fact that the wife he loved deeply had left him for another man. Feeling devastated, he allowed himself to cry freely as he expressed his feelings to a sympathetic friend. A few months later, he told his friend, "The woman I knew and loved is dead, and I'm going to have a funeral for her. I don't know the strange woman who is walking around in her body and wearing her clothes."

It was a mock funeral, of course, carried out in detail in the man's own mind, but it helped him accept his loss and make the first step toward recovery.

Therapists sometimes use the mock funeral, good-bye letters or the Gestalt method to help their clients let go of a past relationship.

A "good-bye letter" should include as many details as possible of both the positive and negative sides of the relationship. For example:

Dear George,
This is good-bye. I'm sorry you died and I miss a lot of things we used to do together. I miss little things like reading the *New York Times* together on Sunday mornings and important things like the support you always gave me. I'm also saying good-bye to your aggravating habit of steaming up the bathroom every morning and that snorting sound you made at night that always kept me awake.

Recalling trivial things helps the writer lead up to more emotional issues—perhaps saying good-bye to a planned child or to dreams of a new house.

Using the Gestalt method, the person imagines talking to the lost mate. Sitting and facing an empty chair, the person envisions the absent spouse and says good-bye, again recalling as many details of the marriage as possible. Going through these exercises can be painful, evoking feelings of anxiety, anguish, and tears; a skilled therapist can make it easier.

THE IMPORTANCE OF ATTITUDE

The report of a disaster on the evening news usually includes brief interviews with several of the victims.

"I'm wiped out," one person will say. "Everything I've built up is gone. I guess this is the end."

Invariably, another victim will say, "The house is gone, but we're so lucky to be alive. We're going to start rebuilding the house as soon as we can."

Joyce DeHaan and Gerard Fisher, of the Center for Organization Development, use these reactions in stress management seminars as examples to illustrate the importance of attitude in managing stress.

"Stress itself is neutral, neither positive nor negative," DeHaan points out. "We have the power to turn stress into negative 'distress' or positive energy."

The widowed or divorced person might say, "I can't go on," "My life is a mess," or, "Since John left, I don't have any friends."

DeHaan and Fisher call these "paralyzing statements" because they sap energy and immobilize the individual. People who believe they "can't go on" probably will go on—but only with great difficulty.

When a person begins to identify some of these paralyzing statements and replace them with what DeHaan and Fisher call "harnessing statements," the energy generated by stress is released. Typical harnessing statements would be, "Sometimes I find it difficult to go on, but I am," or, "This is an extremely difficult situation. What can I do about it?"

The idea that the way one thinks and looks at things can have a profound influence on one's mental health has been well established by psychiatrists and psychotherapists. Dr. Albert Ellis teaches that it is not an event, but one's "beliefs" about the event, that determine one's reactions to it. According to Ellis, thinking patterns can be changed by "disputing irrational beliefs."

This is the basis of cognitive therapy. According to Dr. David D. Burns, author of *Feeling Good: The New Mood Therapy*, anxiety and depression are caused by illogical, negative thinking, which in turn causes self-defeating behavior. Burns's book describes how to diagnose depression and illustrates simple ways of changing thinking patterns to decrease or eliminate anxiety and depression.

ACTIVE COPING

When Mark Trowbridge first learned that his wife, Connie, had cancer, he did two things. He took up running and he started a journal.

"Physical activity is very, very important when you're under a lot of stress," Mark said, recalling how he pushed himself along in the steamy Dallas heat for eight summers. "When I got too tired to run, I walked."

Mark's wife, Connie, died eight years after her disease was first diagnosed. She went through all the stages of grief, Mark said, and he went through them with her—first the denial that this terrible disease had struck a vibrant, healthy woman; then the intense, raging anger at God for letting some misplaced, mysterious organism go awry.

Connie's doctors recommended chemotherapy, and for months they bargained. Let her respond to the treatment. Give her a little more time. Let her live to see her grandchildren.

"It was almost a classic case of the grief stages," Mark said. "In the end, there was almost a . . . almost a willingness."

Connie's disease hovered over them constantly for eight years.

"It grinds you down," Mark said. "I knew if I sat in a room and felt sorry for myself, I could never live through it."

As the southwestern regional manager of a large corporation, Mark was self-assured and confident in the business world. He was a good listener and an entertaining conversationalist at social events. But he had never felt comfortable expressing his personal feelings—in some ways not even to Connie.

"I felt the need to verbalize," Mark said. "But I had no confidante, no intimate friend."

Mark bought a bound journal in a stationery store and started writing in it.

"I would ask myself questions and try to answer them. I would write out little scenarios of what might happen and what I would do. It became almost hypnotic."

By the time Connie was admitted to the hospital for the last time, Mark had filled eight journals, one for each year. During those last months, Mark stopped going to his office regularly and visited Connie several times during the day. Sometimes she recognized him.

Mark wrote the final scenario in his journal as he sat by Connie's bedside on a rainy night.

"I wrote down everything. I made a list of the people who would have to be called and who would do the calling. I decided on a funeral home and wrote down the name and number of the person to contact. I made notes on the service. I wrote out the newspaper obituary."

Connie died quietly without regaining consciousness.

"No. There was no shock," Mark said, shaking his head. "I had already felt the shock when the cancer was first diagnosed. By the time she died, I knew what was going to happen, and I was prepared for it."

In this respect, Mark was unusual. Most widows and widowers we interviewed, even those whose mates died after a long illness when death seemed inevitable, were not really prepared for the shock.

After Connie's death, Mark set his time frame. He decided to postpone making any decisions regarding his future plans for two years. He continued running every day and immersed himself in his work.

The benefits of exercise for the relief of stress and depression have been well documented.

"Exercise is probably the strongest antidepressant we have," writes Jane Fonda in *Women Coming of Age*. She notes, "Many psychiatrists are regularly prescribing exercise as a powerful drug-free therapy for their depressed patients."

While most recent research has focused on running or other aerobic exercises that require an increased oxygen intake, a study at the University of Rochester indicates that other types of exercise, such as weight lifting, are also therapeutic.

Fitness programs are usually based on exercising three times a week for an hour, including the warm-up and cool-down. The aerobics part of the workout usually takes from twenty to thirty minutes, and the goal is to get the heartbeat up from its resting rate to about 75 percent of its maximum rate. It's important to know the minimum and maximum rates, usually based on age, and to take a pulse check before, during, and after working out.

Mark had the right idea, but running every day and in excessive heat may have been overdoing it. It's generally agreed that the body needs a day to rest between strenuous workouts.

DANGER SIGNALS

Feelings of depression, moodiness, thoughts of suicide are natural reactions to the loss of one's mate. The body may in fact even show some physical symptoms of acute distress.

If the symptoms persist over a prolonged period of time or interfere with the normal activities of daily life, professional help is probably needed.

The warning signs that stress levels are reaching the danger point are quite clear, but unfortunately they're easy to ignore. Everyone gets a headache now and then, and an upset stomach can be brushed off as the penalty for ordering "everything" on the pizza last night. Drinking too much once or twice a year doesn't make a person an alcoholic. Feeling annoyed by a traffic jam or a long line at the supermarket is a normal reaction.

But when the headaches become frequent, when mild annoyance turns into outbursts of rage, when drinking too much becomes a regular thing, it's time to do something.

Feelings of anxiety, difficulty sleeping, loss of appetite, or compulsive eating are other common symptoms. Waking up at an early hour with a racing pulse, as several people described in interviews, is a classic.

According to the National Institutes of Mental Health, possible signs of depression include changes in appetite, shifts in sleeping patterns, tiring easily or lacking energy, agitation or increased activity, loss of interest in daily activities, a decreased sex drive, inability to concentrate, feelings of sadness or self-reproach, recurring thoughts of suicide.

If at least four of these symptoms persist, the institutes suggest professional help.

A complete physical examination is a good place to start. The doctor may prescribe a vitamin supplement, particularly vitamin B_6, during the mourning period. Vitamin deficiencies have been connected to depression, although it isn't clear whether this is a direct result of the depression or reflects generally poor nutrition during stressful periods.

If physical illness is ruled out, the next step is an evaluation and treatment by a mental health professional.

A VIEW FROM THE COUCH

Sara Johnston lay back on the psychiatrist's soft, brown leather couch and concentrated on her feet.

"Study the pattern of tension in those muscles, then relax them one by one," the doctor told her. "Breathe deeply. Feel those tiny muscles relaxing more and more."

This was Sara's third appointment with Dr. Michael Brandon. Her internist had referred her after giving Sara a complete physical examination that found her in good physical health. Her recurring dizzy spells were not caused by an inner ear problem. The tightening feeling and extreme pressure she sometimes felt along the back of her head were not caused by a brain tumor or an aneurysm. The palpitations and heart pounding she had come to dread were not the warning signs of an impending heart attack.

"You seem to be having some symptoms of anxiety," her internist had said, and had recommended Dr. Brandon.

Sara had canceled her first two appointments with the psychiatrist. Half the people she knew had been in therapy at one time or another. There was no longer a stigma attached to seeing a psychiatrist, no longer an association with mental illness. Still, Sara kept thinking, I should be able to lick this myself.

Then Sara had a scare. She had an anxiety attack in her car on the way to work. It was her most dreaded fear, to pass out and cause a terrible accident. Cars were speeding along on both sides. Her heart pounded. Her head was spinning. Sara gripped the steering wheel, then managed to pull into the right lane and off the road. She rested her head on the steering wheel. She was sweating, shaking.

"You're at a tennis match and it's a beautiful day. You can feel the warmth of the sun on your back," Dr. Brandon was saying. "Bounce your eyes gently back and forth, following the tennis ball. Feel the muscles work, relaxing the tension.

Study the sensation as the muscles in your eyes continue to relax."

The doctor had prescribed the drug Xanax, .25 mg, three times a day, and he was teaching her relaxation techniques. The drug would reduce the anxiety symptoms but not eliminate them.

At Dr. Brandon's suggestion, Sara had been reading Dr. Claire Weekes's books on anxiety and agoraphobia. Weekes's studies have shown it isn't the anxiety but the fear of an anxiety attack that incapacitates. Weekes calls this the "second fear."

"Learn to loosen your body and accept the anxiety," Dr. Brandon said as Sara rose to leave. "Don't tense up or force yourself and you'll move through it."

Sara nodded.

She walked out to her car, aware of the sun glistening on fresh snow and the clear blue sky, and she drove away feeling better than she had in a long time.

Sara's psychiatrist diagnosed her problem as a form of agoraphobia, from the Greek word *agora,* meaning "fear of the marketplace." In extreme cases, the person is unable to leave the house.

A phobia is a severe anxiety reaction to a situation, animal, or object that poses no real threat to life or safety. The panic attacks usually come out of the blue during a time of generalized psychological stress.

In Sara's case, the psychiatrist helped to educate her on the nature of the problem. The combination of therapy and a mild drug proved successful.

Despite the severe psychological stress that often accompanies a divorce, fewer than 10 percent of the people going through one seek professional counseling. The figure is thought to be even lower among the widowed.

Sara's conviction that she should be able to overcome her problem herself is fairly common. Moreover, there is often confusion over how to find the right professional help.

A medical doctor, clergyman, or lawyer already aware of the circumstances can usually refer the person to a competent professional. Generally speaking, a psychiatrist is appropriate if the problem requires medication. Psychologists deal with emotional and behavioral problems usually not requiring medication. Marriage therapists specialize in family and marital problems. Social workers are often trained both in psychology and marital counseling. Personal referrals to particular professionals are helpful because there is a great deal of overlapping.

A mental health professional can provide crisis intervention for any immediate problems such as mild depression or feelings of being overwhelmed. Over the long term, therapy is usually the answer. With it the person can gain insights into such areas as interaction of the marriage, unresolved conflicts from their own family relationships, and unresolved grief.

The client should feel free to ask ahead of time about fees, what a typical session will be like, who will be included in the therapy, an estimate on the average number of sessions, the policy on telephone calls, and a backup in case the therapist isn't available.

The background and experience of a therapist are important, but probably the most crucial factor is trust. The client must feel comfortable with the therapist. In any long-term therapy, client and therapist must have the same goals. The client is playing the game, the therapist is the coach.

Despite Ann Landers' repeated advice, "Get professional help," she also warns, "The chances of getting a good therapist are about the same as getting a good auto mechanic or a good plumber—about fifty-fifty."

Actually, changing therapists is more difficult than changing auto mechanics because of the personal nature of the relationship. The client should express any doubts about the treatment to the therapist and, if not satisfied, feel free to change.

The widowed are more likely to seek help from the clergy than from mental health professionals, according to Ruth Loewinsohn, author of *Survival Handbook for Widows*. But many ministers have had little formal training in death and bereavement, Loewinsohn notes. One study showed that only 3 percent of widows who sought help felt they received any from the clergy, and only 6 percent felt mental health professionals helped them.

"There is a great need for the education of the unwidowed so they can begin to understand what life is like for the grieving person," Loewinsohn concludes.

TELLING YOUR STORY

Frank Gardener brushed off the suggestion that he get professional help.

"I don't want anything to do with shrinks," Frank said, shaking his head.

Frank lingered over his beer in the neighborhood bar where he had stopped off for a drink after work. He dreaded going back to his tiny apartment and usual solitary dinner. Most of the regulars had already left, and Frank was talking to Daisy, the skinny blonde who tended bar. He was thinking about asking her out.

"Listen, this guy's not a shrink," Daisy said. "He's a counselor. He helped me, and you sure need help."

Frank glanced at his reflection in the mirror behind the bar. The thin, sallow face stared lifelessly back at him.

"You're probably right, Daisy," he said with a sigh, tossing a bill on the counter and putting on his coat. He didn't really want to ask Daisy out.

One morning the following week, after a sleepless night, Frank called Daisy's counselor and made an appointment.

"Where's the anger?"

Frank had just told his story, and John Halloren, a family and marriage counselor, was putting him on the spot.

Frank shook his head. "I don't know."

Halloren recommended two books he thought might help Frank understand some of his feelings about the divorce. He also suggested that Frank start a journal.

Frank carried the books in his briefcase and tried to concentrate on reading them at night in bleak, impersonal hotel rooms. He started a journal, but he had difficulty expressing his feelings. The first entries were rambling:

> Expectations, capabilities, directions or goals. All come to the surface when emotions run. Evaluate, reevaluate your position after a loss. All that was to be important seems to be somewhat empty without a sense of sharing. As it began with a flash it has ended in the same manner. When we met all I could think of was Jill. Now her spirit has left and I'm feeling very empty.

How could he ever feel angry with Jill? He had felt this emptiness after his mother died. He had felt abandoned, as he did now. He hadn't felt angry.

"You may be connecting your mother's death with Jill leaving you," John Halloren said when Frank went in for his appointment the following week. "They left on the same day."

Frank shifted in his chair, feeling uncomfortable.

Frank canceled his next appointment and didn't go back to the counselor. But he became fascinated with writing in his journal. He wrote at random about events in his life and thoughts he would never have felt comfortable expressing to anyone, including the counselor. Even his handwriting had become more even and regular when he wrote:

I'm beginning to realize Jill and I were different from the beginning. We should have remained good friends. Our marriage was a mistake.

Mark Trowbridge had used his journal to fulfill his need to verbalize, and writing in it had come naturally.

Frank found it difficult to express himself, although writing in the journal helped to focus on some issues that had been bothering him.

There are several reasons for keeping a journal during a highly stressful period. An anxiety state usually results in convoluted thinking. People under stress may not be able to "think straight." Writing forces them to focus and to expand their thoughts.

Second, as they describe events in a journal, they are "telling their story." In the case of divorce, the journal can serve as an "account" of what went wrong in the marriage.

This account is of major psychological importance, according to sociologist Robert S. Weiss. It may include significant events that dramatize what went wrong, or it may point up a few themes that ran through the marriage. The account allocates blame for the failure of the marriage among the self, the spouse, and any third party. It also gives the marital separation a plot structure with a beginning, middle, and end. Once the events are understood in this way, the person can begin to deal with them.

The account doesn't have to be absolutely accurate to be useful. The wife's version would probably differ from the husband's account of the same marital separation.

Finally, a journal can help the person go back to the "triggering event." Studies of catastrophe victims indicate that the recovery process can't begin until the person is able to face and relive the original event. This can be painful, but coming to grips with the triggering event is like grabbing the end of a ball of string: only then can the person begin to unravel it.

WITH GOD'S HELP

Judy Carpenter had just returned from seven weeks at a rehabilitation clinic for alcoholics in Minnesota.

"My divorce didn't make me an alcoholic," Judy said as soon as we were settled on a sunny bench in Central Park. "My divorce gave me an excuse to drink."

The announcement sounded like something Judy had memorized, but it rang sincere. The subtle change in her was difficult to pinpoint.

Judy had gained a little weight, but she looked healthy and fit in her bright yellow-and-white knit outfit. The sparkle that had characterized the carefree Judy of earlier days had been replaced by a more thoughtful, serious demeanor. With almost no emotion, Judy talked about the unhappiness and frustration she had gone through as she'd fought to deny that she was an alcoholic.

Judy had hidden her drinking problem from her faculty friends and students in Boulder, and she'd continued to hide it after she had moved to New York City.

"I never missed a day of work, and I never had more than two drinks at parties," Judy said. "What my friends didn't know was that I had four drinks at home before I went to the party. I even developed a drinking vocabulary. I knew there were certain words I couldn't say without slurring. I knew when to slip off my shoes so I wouldn't start tripping over everything."

Then Judy started having blackouts—waking up in the morning unable to remember what had happened the night before.

"I'd check to see if my car was in the garage," she said,

frowning slightly. "Then I'd look it over to see if there were any dents in it. I became so afraid I'd kill myself or someone else. The most frightening part was that I couldn't seem to stop.

"I've heard people say alcoholics have to hit bottom, lose everything before they can be helped, but that isn't true. You can be helped anytime you decide you've had enough."

Judy decided she'd had enough one morning when she woke up on the bathroom floor. Kristen was standing over her with a look of horror on her face.

"Mom, you're hurt. Do you want me to call the doctor?"

Judy lifted her hand and found it covered with blood. Her head ached. As she pulled herself up, Judy saw that the bathroom was covered with bloodstains. There were jagged pieces of a broken wineglass on the floor.

"Luckily, it was just a surface head cut that bled a lot," Judy said. "I realized I could have killed myself. More important than that, I'll never forget the expression on Kristen's face. I finally saw what I was putting her through."

Judy went to her supervisor that morning before she had time to reconsider. She told her that she had a drinking problem and needed help.

"At first she couldn't believe me. She agreed to refer me to a chemical dependency clinic for an evaluation, but she was sure they would tell me I didn't have a problem. The fact is, they told me I needed to get into treatment immediately."

Judy's company medical plan covered her treatment at the clinic. She was there for seven weeks, two weeks longer than the other patients she met there.

"It was tough," Judy recalled. "The atmosphere was like a hospital, and we were on a strict schedule. They divided us into groups, and if we didn't take a pill on time or show up for a meal or therapy session on time, we'd get a reprimand. I'd balk at the regimen sometimes, and the group would get really tough with me. They called me a real phony. The other people in my group said I pretended to be so perfect. They accused me of never showing my real feelings."

At the end of the fifth week, the other members of Judy's group went home, but Judy's therapist decided Judy wasn't ready. In her second group, Judy said she was finally able to confront her feelings.

"I felt worthless, and that was hard for me to accept. I was putting up a front. I thought if people knew what I was really like, they wouldn't have anything to do with me."

Admission of her weakness and frailty had taken Judy through a dark valley. She came through it and survived only by accepting the fact that she wasn't alone.

"For me, it's my belief in God," Judy said. "But I didn't know anyone there who didn't come to believe in some higher power. I think you have to believe in something bigger and more powerful than yourself. The burden gets too heavy. You have to learn to turn it over."

After her release from the clinic, Judy started attending Alcoholics Anonymous meetings every evening after work and during the day on weekends.

"I pray every morning for the strength to get through the day without drinking," Judy concluded. "I thank God every night that I made it. I'm living a day at a time. It's not a bad way to live, alcoholic or not."

For the first time, it struck me that Judy had been alone for a long time.

Judy found the support she needed in Alcoholics Anonymous. One of the largest anonymous groups in the world, A.A. has more than 1,000,000 members in 110 countries. There are no dues or fees, and the only requirement for membership is the desire to stop drinking.

Judy went into A.A. following a rehabilitation program,

but members also join through referrals or on their own. People who think they have a drinking problem or who want information can call the A.A. office listed in most local telephone directories or write the General Service Office, Box 459, Grand Central Station, New York, N.Y. 10163.

WHY ME, LORD?

Under the support of A.A., Judy turned to God for help when she recognized her serious drinking problem as the main aspect of her life over which she had become powerless.

A life crisis seems to force most people to examine, perhaps reexamine, their faith in God or a higher power.

"We had always had a strong faith and tried to raise our children in that faith," Laura Cunningham said. "When David died, I couldn't understand why God was punishing me. Why me?"

One way to make sense out of our suffering is to believe that we somehow get what we deserve, that misfortune is a punishment. So writes Rabbi Harold S. Kushner in *When Bad Things Happen to Good People*. Victims sometimes try to console themselves by concluding that God must have His reasons. Perhaps He is trying to teach the sufferers a lesson or make them better, more sensitive people. Such reasoning is based on the assumption that God wants them to suffer and it is up to them to figure out the reason.

Rabbi Kushner, forced to face this issue when his three-year-old son, Aaron, was diagnosed as having progeria, or "rapid aging," initially reacted the way most people do.

"This can't be happening. This is not how the world is supposed to work."

As he struggled with the question, Rabbi Kushner couldn't accept the idea that God judges people, then passes out punishments and rewards accordingly. By the time his son died at the age of fourteen, Rabbi Kushner had accepted the idea that we live in a less than perfect world, that God cannot prevent suffering, but that He *can* provide the strength and courage to get through it.

People who accept this view can stop asking, "God, why are you doing this to me?" Instead, they can say, "God, something bad has happened. Will you give me the strength to do something about it?"

SUPPORT GROUPS

A dozen women and three men were seated informally around Jan Avery's living room. A couple of the younger women, dressed casually in blue jeans, sat cross-legged on the floor. Ranging in age from late twenties to early sixties, the group appeared to have little in common except the fact that each of them was separated, divorced, or widowed.

"Money," one woman spoke up. "I hate to say it, but that seems to be all I think about. How long can I keep up with the bills? How am I going to send the kids to college?"

Several people in the group nodded understandingly and smiled. Money was a familiar topic. If this turned out to be a typical meeting, however, their stories about money would lead them onto other side roads.

As the group leader for the evening, Jan would try to keep the talk from dead-ending and tactfully draw the quiet ones into the conversation.

For many of them, the group was the one place they could talk openly about their problems and concerns without feeling like complainers. It was comforting to know that others had the same feelings and could understand. It was helpful to hear their suggestions on how they had worked something out.

Jan had volunteered to help the assistant minister of her church organize a support group for the widowed and divorced. Sailing along in her career and personal life, Jan had had a brain aneurysm and her life had come to a screeching halt, almost stopped. She had recovered, but her doctor had told her what she already knew: she couldn't go back to work.

"I needed to do something, and this was one thing I could do," Jan said. "I've been there myself. If nothing else, I could offer them hope. I could let them know they could feel good about their lives again."

Jan had "been there" three times. Her first, youthful marriage had ended in divorce. Her second husband had died of a heart attack when he was only thirty-two. Jan's third marriage had ended in divorce when she was in her early forties. "All I could see then was that I was a three-time loser. I didn't think I'd ever get over it."

Jan has shared her experiences with the group. She has told her often humorous stories of resuming a career after forty, the ups and downs of being a single mother, the slow recovery of self-esteem.

"Money is a primary concern for most of the divorced women in the group, particularly during the first year," Jan said. "The widowed tend to berate themselves for not making more of an effort during the marriage, for not letting their loved one know they cared."

Although she could empathize, Jan cautioned, "Never tell a person you know how they feel. You can't know how another person feels. You can listen. You can let them know you care."

ONE-TO-ONE HELP FOR THE WIDOWED

The widowed, particularly men, are often reluctant to join a support group or to reach out to their family and friends for the help they need. The Widowed Persons Service (WPS), established by the American Association of Retired Persons (AARP) in 1973, has a one-to-one outreach program for the widowed in 170 communities, with about forty new programs being added annually.

"We don't wait for the widowed to come to us," said Ruth Loewinsohn of the AARP in Washington, D.C. "We go to them."

WPS helps organize the programs, but each one is community-based and staffed by volunteers. Getting the names of the widowed from newspaper obituaries and funeral directors, volunteers make personal contact and try to help the widowed through the initial adjustments.

If there is no local program, the WPS puts the widowed in touch with services available in their community on such matters as housing adjustments, family relations, and legal affairs.

Despite the help available, an AARP study showed participation in self-help groups is less than one man to ten women. Yet for every three women who become widows every year, two men are widowed.

The AARP appointed a task force to study the problems of widowed men, and its findings were grim. Compared to married men of the same age, widowers die four times as often from suicide, three times as often from automobile accidents, ten times as often from strokes, and six times as often from heart disease.

Although 52 percent of widowed men remarry within eighteen months after the death of their wives, more than half of these marriages end in divorce, according to AARP figures.

The task force made several proposals for reaching these "forgotten men," including more programs of special interest to men and asking more men to serve on WPS boards.

The emotional recovery from the loss of one's mate involves difficult, painful work. Denying or refusing to work through one's grief can impair growth and development.

The grieving person can do a number of things to make the work easier.

First, an understanding of the grief process helps decrease the feelings of fear and panic that come with not knowing what to expect. Grief is normal and natural. By accepting this fact, one can begin to focus on specific tasks such as saying good-bye to the loved one and acknowledging that a period in one's life has ended.

The path to recovery is not a straight-line progression, as Laura learned. One should except and prepare for setbacks. Laura might have written out a modus operandi for emergencies in advance and carried it in her purse or tacked it to the refrigerator. Her m.o. might have included (1) call Nancy, (2) take a bubble bath, and (3) have a banana split (or any activity that normally made her feel better).

Second, the bereaved must be aware that changes cause stress and that they are going through an extremely stressful period in their lives. They can prevent stress from becoming distress by taking steps to improve both their physical and mental health.

Mark chose running, and Laura signed up for an exercise class. Any fitness program, preferably including aerobic exercise, can help relieve the tension caused by stress.

Good mental health is equally important. In times of stress, the mind seems to dwell on negatives. Once these illogical, destructive thoughts are identified, they can be changed to logical, constructive ideas.

Keeping a journal can be a valuable tool during periods of great stress. Mark used his journal as confidante and friend, satisfying his need to verbalize. Writing helped Frank to focus his thinking and, eventually, to unload the feelings he had been holding in.

Finally, the grieving person must have supportive, appropriate help. Family and friends may be too emotionally involved or too inexperienced to fill the need. An appropriate support group or mental health professional may be the answer.

Sara felt helpless and frightened by her anxiety attacks. When she understood the reason for them and started in treatment, her fears lost the control they had held over her.

Judy found the help she needed in A.A. and learned a valuable lesson. Sometimes the strongest people need help. She also learned that she was not alone.

8: THE OLDER SINGLE

When someone close to us is widowed or divorced, we encourage them to form new relationships and to try new experiences. They must start over, build a new life.

We're likely to take a different viewpoint if the newly single person is Dad or Mom. We tend to put our parents into a special category of people with specific, rather narrow roles.

Whatever qualities parents may have, their children see them primarily as caretakers and authority figures. Children may leave home, rebel, or even turn hostile about their upbringing, but this primary image of their parents usually persists into adulthood.

The generation gap is a chasm some parents and children never cross. They condescendingly talk about "in your day" and "in my day" as if unaware that customs and mores change but basic human needs remain essentially the same.

When one parent dies, the children may be keenly aware of their own loss but fail to recognize the full meaning of the loss to the widowed parent.

"When my dad died, I was all wrapped up in my own grief and loss," said a thirty-four-year-old woman. "I helped my mother make the funeral arrangements and send out the thank-you notes, but I didn't really think about what she was personally going through."

The death of a parent can be a symbolic passing of the torch. A fifty-four-year-old man told me of the experience of being escorted to the front row of the church at his father's funeral on the arm of his own son. His son had whispered, "Dad, you've graduated. You're in the front row now."

The front row, the head of the line.

"I sat there thinking about the responsibility," the man said. "I was the oldest son, and I realized I'd be responsible for my mother from now on. The family would look to me when there was a major decision to be made."

The elderly or ailing widowed parent may have to rely on his or her children for care or financial help, a role reversal that can create tension, guilt, and problems for everyone involved. But this is not the norm.

Spouses become widows or widowers at the average age of fifty-six, according to a study by the American Association of Retired Persons. A healthy fifty-six-year-old is, in many ways, enjoying the prime of life. Having raised their children, worked hard at careers, perhaps accumulated their share of material possessions, people in their late fifties can look forward to a time to reassess, set new goals, and lead richer, more satisfying lives.

"A whole new social era stretches out before we become physically old," writes Dr. Estelle Fuchs in *The Second Season*, a reassuring look at life for women after menopause.

With improved health and medical care, people can look forward to living longer than past generations. The over-sixty-five segment of the population has already reached 20 million and is expected to rise to 26 million by the year 2000.

Longer life expectancy puts a different meaning on the "till death do us part" clause in the marriage vows. A couple who got married in 1900 could expect death to part them in about twenty years. The high death rate from childbirth meant a man could have two or three wives in the cemetery plot before he himself died at a relatively early age.

Now a couple can expect to celebrate their golden fiftieth anniversary in good health, even though an increasing number are deciding to leave before the party.

The period after the youngest child leaves home is one of the critical periods in a marriage. Very often satisfaction with the marriage is at a low point, research shows. In fact, today's fastest-rising divorce rate is in this age group.

The divorce of an older couple may baffle, even embarrass their grown children. Why would a couple who stayed together for twenty years or more suddenly decide to get a divorce?

The most obvious factor is the so-called empty nest syndrome. After the last child leaves home, the couple is alone, face to face, often for the first time in years. If identity has rested on child rearing for either or both, they may suddenly feel like strangers. Often the crux is less a matter of the children leaving home than a resurgence of old problems the couple repressed while putting their energies into raising their family.

Middle age is often the time when priorities change. The father who has devoted himself to work may have reached the mentor stage in his career. Work isn't everything. He may be seeking more intimacy in a love relationship, placing more value on friendships.

At the same time, the mother may be placing more emphasis on her career or resuming a career she interrupted to raise her children.

Unless the couple can renegotiate, the marriage may be in trouble.

If the marriage breaks up in divorce, the couple's adult

children may feel torn. Should the children be newly married or thinking about getting married, they may feel threatened. If their parents couldn't make their marriage last, can they?

Sometimes adult children feel forced to take sides against the parent who initiated the divorce. How could Dad leave Mom after all these years? Will we have to take care of her? What happens to the inheritance?

At the least, a midlife divorce breaks up the family portrait. The younger couple who looked forward to taking their children "over the meadow and through the woods to Grandmother's house" for the holidays may now have to plan a second trip to visit Grandfather and his new bride.

A NEW IDENTITY

Laura Cunningham's first date after her husband died convinced her she could live without a social life. A wrestling match in the front seat of a car might be an interesting exercise during the teenage years but hardly befitted a mature woman.

Her friend Greta was trying to convince Laura she should get out of the house more. Greta, a buyer in housewares at the department store, went to Saturday night dances at the Elks Club and related gossipy tidbits on Monday mornings.

"You'd enjoy it," she told Laura one Monday morning. "It's not a dating kind of thing, just people our age having a good time."

Seated at a small table in the department store's chrome-and-white-Formica coffee shop, Laura and Greta were taking their fifteen-minute morning break from housewares. Laura smiled; she admired Greta's openness and enthusiasm. A homely woman with hawklike features, Greta had been the first to welcome Laura at the store. On that first day, when Laura had felt uncertain, Greta had asked her to lunch.

"Not that I'd be going if you had to have a date," Greta

said with a trace of chagrin. "When I was a kid, my mother told me not to worry about not being pretty. She said looks aren't important if you're neat and clean. I believed her until I was eighteen. Then I figured out why boys weren't asking me out."

Laura laughed. "I'll go with you sometime," she said, glancing up at the big round clock. "We'd better get back."

Greta interpreted "sometime" as Saturday night. As they were leaving the store on Wednesday, Greta offered to pick Laura up. On Thursday morning, Greta suggested they spend their lunch hour shopping for a new dress for Laura.

"Are you sure it's me?"

Laura eyed herself critically in the full-length mirror in the tiny dressing room. The soft printed silk dress with a deep neckline had been Greta's choice. Laura had to admit the dress was feminine and pretty, flattering to her new aerobically shaped figure.

"No, it isn't," Greta admitted, then added confidently, "But it's going to be."

The Elks Club hall was already crowded when Laura and Greta arrived that Saturday night. As they stood in line at the door, Laura noticed that the people ahead of them were paying for their tickets and holding a hand out to get it stamped. She remembered high school dances in the gymnasium with streamers and balloons.

"Come," Greta urged. "I want you to meet some people."

Greta seemed to know almost everyone at the dance. After the first few hurried introductions, Laura stopped trying to put the names and faces together. She was relieved when the band started to play an old Glenn Miller song and the crowd started to disperse to the dance floor. With a little wave, Greta glided onto the dance floor with her partner.

Laura wended her way to the buffet and asked for a cup of wine punch. The cup solved the problem of what to do with her hands, and she stood watching the couples on the dance floor. Yes, it was just like high school, Laura decided. The vivacious gray-haired woman had surely been the beauty queen. The balding hulk had been a football player. Along the sidelines were the wallflowers.

"I'd offer you a penny for your thoughts, but they've got to be worth a quarter at least."

Laura jumped self-consciously.

The man standing beside her was smiling, pleasant-looking.

"I'm Bart Kramer," he said, holding out his hand. He was a stocky man, only a few inches taller than Laura, good-looking in a rough-hewn way.

"And why are you so serious in the midst of all this frivolity?" Bart asked after Laura had introduced herself.

When Laura hesitated, Bart went on, "I've never been able to figure out how they can have such a good time when this is the strongest drink in the house."

Bart held up the wine punch cup and frowned.

"It's a nice party," Laura said, wishing she didn't feel so tongue-tied.

The announcer's voice, magnified and distorted by a faulty microphone, cut the conversation short.

"Ladies on the left, gents on the right."

Bart took Laura's punch cup and made a flourishing gesture toward the dance floor. The line dances were drawing everyone onto the floor. Laura found herself laughing at the mix-ups that invariably followed the announcer's instructions to change steps.

Bart suddenly appeared opposite her in the line. As they passed each other, he asked, "Do you feel like we're back in kindergarten?"

"Now we'll have a ladies' choice," the announcer blared. "Come on, ladies. Don't be shy."

Laura glanced around the room. Bart was watching her. Flustered, Laura asked the nearest man to dance, a thin fellow named Harold who seemed delighted by the offer. He stepped on Laura's feet repeatedly and apologized profusely each time.

"I saw you talking to Bart Kramer," Greta said on the way home. "When he shows up, he's usually the life of the party—a big drinker, a big joker. Everyone says his wife got tired of the drinking. They say he went home one day and she was gone. I wouldn't encourage him if I were you."

Laura wasn't sure why, but she wished she had asked Bart to dance during the ladies' choice.

A DAUGHTER'S VIEW

Laura's married daughter, Anne Munson, had an image of how a widowed grandmother should behave, and her mother wasn't fitting into the image.

"At first, we couldn't get her to do anything," Anne said. "Now, she's making a fool of herself. My brother and I could have helped her financially, but she took that menial job at the department store. It's embarrassing. At this time in her life, she should be able to enjoy the luxury of sitting back and playing with her grandchildren."

Anne was sincere. She remembered Laura's years of devotion as a full-time mother. Anne remembered the birthday gifts on her breakfast plate, the surprise birthday parties, the egg hunts on Easter morning, the fun of decorating the house for the holidays. Anne had kept up those family traditions for her own children. Why wasn't Laura content to fulfill her role as a loving grandmother?

"She's been going to dances at the Elks Club," Anne said. "I don't remember her caring about dancing while Dad was alive."

Laura had, in fact, gone back to the Elks Club with Greta the following week. When she finally saw Bart standing in the doorway, she knew why she had come. Bart had asked her to dance, and by the end of the evening, she had invited him to her house for dinner on Tuesday evening.

"He's crude," Anne told her bluntly after meeting Bart for the first time. "I don't see why you would want to spend any time with him."

Laura didn't try to defend Bart. She was sometimes embarrassed herself by his repertoire of off-color jokes and his obvious attempts to grab the limelight.

But Laura had seen another side of Bart. When they were alone, he could relax and talk quietly. He seemed to enjoy puttering and fixing things around her house. In fact, for a man who had set records for his consumption of Jack Daniels, Bart seemed surprisingly content to sit on the back porch with Laura and sip iced tea.

Some children don't want their parents to change, and this attitude persists into adulthood. At the same time, adult children are involved with their own lives and families. They usually don't have a lot of time to spend with their parents. The dichotomy can create guilt and dissension on both sides.

Much as she loved her grandchildren, Laura wasn't ready for the rocking chair.

Left alone and forced by circumstances into redefining her identity as a single woman, Laura was venturing into unfamiliar territory. While her daughter saw the clerking job as demeaning, Laura was gaining confidence from proving she could support herself.

Although she didn't share Greta's enthusiasm for the Saturday night dances at the Elks Club, Laura liked the feeling of having "a place to go." She was becoming more at ease socially.

Bart's friendship filled a need that even Laura found difficult to articulate.

"Someone finds me interesting enough to spend time with me," she would occasionally say to herself. Only a person who had been alone could understand how much that meant. She didn't try to explain it to her daughter.

Laura had no desire to remarry, certainly not to Bart. Her goal was to become independent and, in the process, learn to enjoy herself again. Anne, who could have considered those goals quite logical for anyone else, couldn't relate them to her mother.

THE INDEPENDENT PARENT

Evelyn Marchand was elegantly laid out in a soft orchid negligee according to her wishes. Her face in final repose reflected the self-confidence, the determination that had molded the wrinkled countenance in life. At ninety-two, she had outlived her husband, two of her children, and most of her friends.

"She wanted to be independent and she hung in there," said her son, Charles. "She was able to take care of herself, almost to the end."

Evelyn had moved into the English Tudor–style house in Philadelphia at the turn of the century as a bride from the Midwest. Twenty-two at the time, Evelyn had come from a well-to-do family in St. Louis. Her husband, Horace, had been twenty-five and already established in his own architectural business.

To the handful of friends left to mourn her death, Evelyn had had an easy life. A live-in housekeeper, Emma, had run the house for more than forty years. Emma's husband, Clyde, had been the chauffeur and gardener. After driving Horace to his office every morning, Clyde had often been seen waiting outside one of the city's best department stores until Evelyn came out to get his help with her packages.

"I'll never forget what a stir she caused among the women

in the Episcopal church," said an elderly woman who had come to pay her respects. "I had warned her they might be a little snobbish, but Evelyn said she couldn't imagine what they had to be snobbish about."

Evelyn had raised a few eyebrows by drinking bourbon whiskey at elite parties and openly expressing her liberal political views.

"That was nothing to the stir she caused when Emma died and she insisted on burying her in the family plot," Charles recalled. "The cemetery officials didn't mention the fact that it was an all-white cemetery. They avoided that issue and told Mother she couldn't put Emma there because the plot was for family members only. Mother looked them straight in the eye and told them Emma was part of the family and that's where she belonged."

Some said Evelyn had succeeded in getting away with her eccentricities because she had old money behind her. Money, they said, gave people the power to control their destinies. Only a few of her closest friends knew her husband's death in the mid-1950s had plunged her into bankruptcy. Horace was diabetic and had suffered from gout and other complications for years. He had died on the operating table during surgery to amputate his leg.

"Dad thought he was leaving us well off financially, and we didn't tell him differently," Charles said. "The fact is, he left us with more debts than money."

Evelyn had worn an elegant black lace dress to her husband's funeral. Head held high, she'd never reached for the dainty, monogrammed handkerchief she had tucked into her purse. She had mourned her loss deeply, but only her family and close friends shared her tears.

Evelyn's immediate thought had been to save the company. She had started going to the office every day, studying the books and each aspect of the business. Within a few months, she knew it was hopeless.

"I tried to get her to sell the house and move in with us," Charles said. "She wouldn't have any part of it. She said she wasn't going to leave the house until they carried her out feet first."

Close to admitting she was licked, Evelyn hit on an idea. She was attending a cocktail party one evening where a man choked on a glass swizzle stick. He died before the ambulance reached the hospital. While most of the people who attended the party regarded the incident as a horrible freak accident, Evelyn gave it a great deal of thought. The next morning at the office, she looked over some samples of a new material the designers were beginning to incorporate into buildings. She took some pieces home that night and discovered she could bend them after heating them in the oven. Swizzle sticks made from this material could be attractive, lightweight, and safe, Evelyn thought.

"She never did anything on a small scale," Charles said with a smile. "She took her first samples to the swankiest shops in New York City where she had charge accounts and she came home with orders. Frankly, I don't know how we managed to fill them, but the whole family pitched in and we did it."

From plastic swizzle sticks, Evelyn eventually added a full line of bar, bathroom, and home accessories. She worked out methods to mass-produce and hired a small staff of workers.

Eventually she sold her flourishing business to one of her workers who had gradually taken over the day-to-day operation.

"Kitchens are for servants," she told a friend who expressed surprise that Evelyn continued to eat alone in the formal dining room. The "servants" had long since been reduced to a day maid who cleaned, cooked, and tried to keep up the yard and gardens with the help of neighborhood boys wanting odd jobs.

"She was a wonderful example," Charles said. "She always

taught us to aim high and work hard. She said the only person who can defeat you is yourself."

Evelyn's story disputes the gloomy stereotypes of the aging single parent. Her counterparts can be found in all segments of society—older single parents who are functioning well on their own and maintaining good relationships with their adult children.

Regardless of their background or circumstances, people like Evelyn appear to share certain qualities—they seem to enjoy life, and they look for constructive, positive ways to cope.

A woman seated beside a campfire at the Women's Peace Encampment had this quality. Having raised her children and retired from a teaching career, she had become actively involved in the peace movement. A retired man who meets his friends in the park for a game of chess on Saturdays had this quality. Having worked hard at his career for many years, he enjoyed spending time on quality friendships. Older singles who are making the most of this stage in their lives can be found almost anywhere—in the Peace Corps, running marathons, starting second careers, tending gardens.

We envy them their zest for life. Younger people who admired Evelyn's resourcefulness as an aging entrepreneur often remarked, "I hope I can be like that when I'm old." The question, of course, is, Were they "like that" when they were younger?

Studies have shown that, by and large, we keep the same basic traits throughout life. Parents who manipulated their children when they were younger are more likely to manipulate them as adults. Parents who complained about the burdens of parenting will probably complain about the trials and tribulations of growing older. Parents who chose the martyr role are likely to become experts with age.

People do grow and change, but only through effort and work. As Evelyn's story illustrates, facing and overcoming adversity is one way they accomplish this.

THE LONG-DISTANCE WORRY

Failing health and the frailty that eventually comes with old age are among the most complex problems for aging single parents and their children.

"I fell last night, but I don't think I broke any bones."

This kind of telephoned news usually marks the beginning of a new era for children who have supported their parent's effort to remain self-sufficient.

"How did it happen?"

"Did you see a doctor?"

"Which bones?"

Although many adult children have received such calls, this particular call came from an eighty-two-year-old man who had chosen to remain in his home in a small rural community after his wife died. His children supported the idea for several reasons.

Their dad was already in his early seventies when their mother died. He was still in good health and seemed to enjoy keeping up the minimal yardwork. Years before, they had stopped planting vegetable gardens and annual flower gardens.

Most important, their dad knew everyone in the community. He could walk to the store for a few groceries or down to the barber shop to get his hair cut. One of his sons lived only an hour away and agreed to check on Dad once a week.

The arrangement worked out well until the old man had a serious bout of pneumonia one winter.

"I jump every time the telephone rings," his son said. "What if he falls again and this time it's more serious? What if he gets sick? The doctor told him it was important to keep warm, but he keeps the house at fifty degrees. He could afford to turn the heat up, but he says that's wasteful. I try to reason with him. I can't force him."

Many adult children face this dilemma. Is the elderly parent capable of self-care? Should they take the parent into their home and risk upsetting their own family routine? Should they start thinking about a nursing home?

In the meantime, they jump when the telephone rings.

Despite our mobile society, most families do stay strong, connected, and caring even after the children grow up, leave home, and marry. According to one study, 85 percent of people over sixty-five have children living an hour or less away, and only 2 percent hadn't seen any of their children for over a year.

Elderly people live longer, happier lives when they can remain in their own homes and receive special services, according to a study of 4,000 Medicaid recipients over the age of sixty-five in California. These special services include visits from public health nurses, social workers, and volunteers. The services supplement but don't replace the support of families and friends.

Families who want to support a parent's wish to stay at home should check into community resources. In addition to home nursing care, many communities have volunteer programs that provide such services as daily hot meals, a daily telephone check, and help with transportation.

THE NURSING HOME?

When Charles Hartman forgot to turn off the burner on his electric stove one evening and almost burned his house down, his three children and their spouses held a conference.

Charlie's oldest child, Marvin, got right to the point.

"What are we going to do about Dad?"

Although Charlie still had lucid moments, his memory lapses proved what his doctor had been telling his children for some time: at age eighty-four, Charlie was rapidly becoming senile.

"He needs someone to look after him," Marvin went on.

The group was silent. They all knew Marvin was right. Charlie's right leg had never fully mended from a fall down the stairs the previous year. Since then, he'd cut his hand while trying to operate the power lawn mower, and, of course, there was the fire.

"I think you all know I'd be glad to take him into our home," Marvin said, breaking the long silence. "But with both of us working, I don't see how we could do it."

The children had come to Charlie's home, as they did several times a year, for Sunday dinner. Marvin and his wife had brought a baked ham, and the others had provided the vegetables, salad, and Charlie's favorite chocolate cake. If the gathering around the big dining room table had seemed more subdued than usual, Charlie apparently hadn't noticed. He had gone to his room for an afternoon rest, as had become his habit, and the others had gathered in the living room for serious conversation.

"I don't see how I could do it," Charlie's daughter, the middle child, finally spoke up. "I've got my hands full with the kids and we don't really have the room."

Charlie's youngest son, a bachelor who lived some distance away, finally said it. The words had been hanging in the room, waiting to be spoken:

"Maybe we should look into a nursing home."

How many children have deliberated the same issue? They all agree it would be good to know that Dad was getting the care he needed and regular meals. He might even enjoy being among people his age. But would he accept the idea of selling the house, virtually his only asset? And how would they pay for a nursing home when that money ran out?

As others before them have concluded, Charlie's children finally agreed that a nursing home was the only logical solution.

Charlie accepted his children's decision with unexpected stoicism. He packed his clothes and a few personal belongings, looking at his wife's photograph through watery eyes as he carefully placed it in his small case.

During his first few weeks at the home, Charlie refused to leave his tiny room and passed the time watching soap operas or staring out of the window. A volunteer aide finally talked him into taking the crafts class she was teaching in the sunroom twice a week, and he started making woven belts for Christmas presents.

When the class was over, Charlie missed seeing the other residents he had met in the class. He started joining them for weekly church meetings and the occasional programs put on by groups in the area. As the holidays approached, Marvin was encouraged to find his father in better spirits.

When Marvin opened his Christmas present and saw the woven belt, he was overcome with an indescribable sadness. The strapping, hardworking father he remembered from his youth had been reduced to weaving belts.

"I hope it fits," the old man said, clearly pleased by his accomplishment.

The sadness wasn't for his father, Marvin realized. He had just caught a glimpse of his own mortality. Where would he end his days? Who would make that decision?

Whenever possible, the elderly parent should be included in the decision to move into a nursing home and be given an extra measure of support during the transition period. A dramatic change in the pattern of daily life, difficult at any age, can be traumatic for the elderly.

Charlie's children agreed a nursing home was the best option under the circumstances. Rather than include Charlie in their discussion, however, they made the decision and announced their conclusion.

Perhaps they were afraid he wouldn't agree. Perhaps they thought he was too senile. They should have taken the risk. Charlie might have welcomed the prospect of less responsibility at his age. Having a choice in the matter would have given him a feeling of security and made it easier for him to adjust.

Ideally, the elderly parent and children should visit several nursing homes together and talk about the different choices within their financial means.

The nursing home scandals of recent years may have created a negative impression in some people's minds about the quality of nursing home care. The fact that substandard homes exist merely emphasizes the importance of checking on the facilities and care in advance.

The trend has been toward encouraging residents to remain self-sufficient as long as possible. Many nursing homes are designed with kitchenettes. Residents have the option of preparing all or part of their meals or eating in the dining room.

The latest complexes for the elderly include small apartments where residents live independently with medical and other services on the grounds. The resident can feel secure knowing help is close at hand. If necessary, they can move into a full-care facility without leaving familiar surroundings.

When the parent and children plan the move together and attention is focused on the positive aspects, the parent's apprehension can be greatly relieved.

DYING AT HOME

Stella Marche didn't give a thought to a nursing home when her mother, Mary Winston, could no longer take care of herself. A close friend of the family had called Stella from Indiana to express concern about Mary's rapidly declining health.

"I was shocked by how sick and frail she looked in only the few months since I'd been out there," Stella said. "I went into the bedroom and cried."

Tears dried, Stella had taken charge of the situation. She spent a week closing the family home and taking care of her mother's financial matters. Weak and frail, Mary agreed to go home with Stella and stay until she felt stronger. Stella's husband, Jeremy, a retired college professor, had suggested a nursing home, but Stella would have none of it.

The old woman sat propped up by bed pillows in the overstuffed chair. Her feet, encased to the ankles in pink knitted house slippers, were stretched out in front of her on a simulated leather hassock. At ninety-two, Mary Winston had taken on the demeanor of a wizened queen.

"Where's my tea?"

"I'm fixing it, Mother," Stella said, trying to hold back any trace of irritation.

They had just finished the tedious morning ritual of getting Mary out of bed and dressed for the day. As usual, Mary had insisted she didn't need any help, and, as usual, Stella had almost carried the old woman into the bathroom. Mary had spent several minutes picking out the printed voile dress she wanted to wear that day. She had sat on the edge of the bed, a rag doll, while Stella had dressed her; Stella's back now ached from the effort. Stella herself would be seventy in another month. She didn't like to think about it.

Stella served the tea with a thick slice of homemade bread

and strawberry jam, placing the cup and plate carefully on a metal table beside her mother's chair.

"You know I don't like jam," Mary said, frowning.

"You asked me if I had any jam yesterday," Stella reminded her.

The old woman thought for a moment.

"I think I'll go home tomorrow," she said finally.

Home. Stella thought about the two-story frame house in Terre Haute, Indiana, where she had grown up. She remembered her mother in those days, polishing and waxing, always working at something. She had a vivid mental image of coming downstairs on Monday mornings to the steamy odor of white clothes boiling on the wood stove in the kitchen. Her mother, face flushed from the steam, had scrubbed the clothes on a well-worn washboard.

She was really a pretty woman, Stella thought, realizing she hadn't been aware of it at the time.

"I'm going home tomorrow," Mary said again.

"Maybe you could put it off until the end of the week," Stella said gently. "Or maybe next week."

Stella was beginning to hate this constant game playing. Her mother was always threatening to leave. She couldn't tell her she had finally sold the house in Indiana, that she'd had no choice. The house had needed major repairs, and for all the warm memories, Stella and Jeremy hadn't been able to afford the expense.

"I don't like your New Jersey," Mary said petulantly. "I want to go home."

"I know." Stella sighed.

Mary sipped her tea. She had shrunk. The flowered voile dress hung on her shoulders. Her hands trembled slightly, causing the teacup to tinkle against the saucer.

Mary had worked hard in her day. She had been a strong, uncomplaining woman. Stella reminded herself that now it was her turn to be strong, uncomplaining. She cleared the dishes and rinsed them at the sink. When she returned to the living room, Mary had fallen asleep. She looked so fragile, breathing shallowly with her mouth slightly open.

Someday, perhaps soon, the frail body would give out and the old woman would stop breathing. Stella thought about it, prepared herself. She couldn't say, or even think, "I hope it will be soon."

The dutiful child will do almost anything to please his or her parents.

Stella couldn't have turned her aging mother over to strangers without suffering deep feelings of guilt. Look at all her mother had done for her! Now it was her turn, her duty to repay the debt.

Stella hadn't counted on the interest the debt had accrued. Mary became more childlike every day, reverting to attention getting and little power struggles to gain control. She continued her threats to go back to Indiana. She lingered longer and longer over her choice of dress for the day. She demanded some different treat with her tea every morning.

During the last weeks of her life, Mary lost control over her bladder and bowels. She rarely slept through the night. Stella struggled with fatigue and the anguish of watching her mother slowly slipping away.

To Jeremy, Stella's concern for her mother began to seem like an obsession. When he couldn't think of a reason to leave the house, he turned silent or quarrelsome.

Mary died on a cold February morning. Stella had removed Mary's gown and was giving her a warm bath when she became aware of her mother's cold skin. She couldn't find a pulse. She went on with her work. She changed the sheets and dressed her mother in a favorite pink nightgown. Then she went downstairs and asked Jeremy to call the doctor.

Stella refused the Valium her doctor prescribed. She felt a sense of relief and peace.

Stella and Jeremy signed up for a college alumni cruise in the Greek islands that spring. They returned sunburned and healthy. Jeremy said Stella was like "a new person."

Stella had made the decision to take care of her mother in those final days, and she had no regrets. If she had it to do over, Stella said she would have tried to enlist a support system. A visiting nurse, family members, or friends could have given her some relief. Perhaps even Jeremy would have been more supportive if she had tried to explain why this final gift to her mother was important to her.

When older parents are widowed or divorced, adult children should try to accept them as people going through the normal phases of life.

Laura's daughter Anne probably would have understood erratic behavior in a friend who had been recently widowed. If Anne had tried to understand the motivations behind her mother's effort to support herself and to make new connections, she might have found Laura's "menial" job, the dances, and even her mother's friendship with Bart more acceptable.

The gradual role reversal of parents and their children is part of the normal progression of life that adult children often try to deny. Some children want their parents to be the same models they knew from earliest memory—yesterday, today, and tomorrow. They hold on to an illusion that the parent of their early years was strong and wise. It's hard to admit sometimes that the parent was never quite so ideal a person.

Accepting one's parents as human beings with normal strengths and weaknesses opens new possibilities for enhancing the child-parent relationship. Charlie's children might have been able to say, "How can we help, Dad?" instead of, "What are we going to do about Dad?"

If the parent is mentally impaired or terminally ill, the children may have to make some difficult decisions regarding their care.

Hospice care offers a solution for terminally ill patients who want to die at home. It provides both professional care in the home and a support group for the family. The concept started in England in the 1960s and spread to this country in the 1970s. It stems from the Middle Ages, when travelers would stop at places called hospices to rest before continuing their journeys. In hospices, terminally ill patients are helped in their journey from life to death.

The stories of these older parents and their children illustrate the strength of family bonds. Adult children have the power to hurt their parents, as in Laura's story, or to provide loving support, as in Evelyn's case.

9: REJOINING THE WORLD

The clock radio on the bedside table switched on in the middle of a weather report: ". . . another sunny day with a high in the eighties and a low in the sixties . . ."

Sara Johnston rolled over sleepily and pressed the alarm button. The early morning fog was dissipating and sunlight streamed across the foot of her bed. Sara sighed contentedly and turned over, fluffing the down pillow around her head.

The thump of a furry body landing on her foot and the purring of its small engine told Sara that her new kitten wasn't going to let her catch another five minutes.

"Okay, Gomer, I'll get up," Sara said, rubbing her foot against the tiger kitten's soft belly. "I'm ready for my coffee, anyway."

Coming down the stairs from the loft bedroom, Sara looked around the living room of her new townhouse. She loved the warm, sunny colors she had chosen, with no one else to please, and she luxuriated in the freedom of being by herself.

How nice to have my own place, she thought.

Sharing her house with Betsy had worked out well for Sara

in many ways. The extra money had enabled her to postpone going back to school for graduate work until she was ready for it. When Sara had gone back to school, Betsy's presence had been like a tonic as Sara had adjusted to classrooms and studying. After graduation, as she'd settled into a more regular routine at the hospital, Sara had begun to yearn for a place of her own. The house held old memories.

Sara didn't want to go back to apartment living, and houses required too much upkeep. She had loved the small townhouse with its skylights and brick-walled garden from the first moment she'd seen it.

Sara filled the coffeepot and poured some milk into Gomer's bowl.

"There you go. You're hungry this morning."

Sara had discovered the baby tiger kitten hovering near her neighbor's clothes-dryer vent the evening she'd moved in. She had carried the wet, bedraggled kitten from door to door without locating its owner. After a week, she'd stopped making inquiries. She'd admitted, grudgingly at first, that she liked having the kitten there when she got home from work. She talked to it while she fixed her dinner, enjoyed its playfulness.

During the months after Jim had left her, Sara wouldn't have wanted the responsibility of a pet. She could remember facing every day with trepidation. Taking care of herself had been challenge enough.

There were still times when the old anxiety swept over her, but her reaction now was more curious than upset.

"What's happening? Why am I feeling this way?"

Sara was aware of her growing self-confidence. She was proud of herself for getting through her graduate studies and surprised that she had been able to keep up with the younger students.

Her new job as an administrative assistant at the hospital

had been challenging and hard at first, but Sara was beginning to relax and enjoy it. In confronting new situations almost every day, she was learning. She had become more forgiving of herself when she made mistakes.

Sara's new job didn't leave her much time for socializing. The wide circle of acquaintances she had known while she was married to Jim had been replaced by a few close friends she had met through her work. Big parties had been replaced by informal dinners with two or three people.

"I haven't been asked," she told a friend at the hospital who wondered why Sara never dated.

She thought about it sometimes. She thought about how good it would be to be with a man. When the urge came, she had learned to explore the warm, silken recesses of her body, to enjoy the rush of warm waves that released the tension.

Gomer padded around the bedroom as Sara finished dressing for work, rubbing against her leg as she filled his dish with dry cat food.

Sara picked up her briefcase, taking a last glance in the foyer mirror. She was looking forward to her day.

Sara had managed to work through her grief and to emerge as a more complete person. She had learned to make decisions on her own and to manage her life with a fair degree of success. Overall, she was content.

Divorce therapist Bruce Fisher refers to this stage of contentment as the "singleness" stage. At this point, the person builds confidence and begins to enjoy being single as an alternate life-style. A person who is comfortable being single can get stuck, using the good life as an excuse for avoiding another relationship, Fisher wrote in *Rebuilding,* but the person who has achieved self-confidence is, in fact, prepared for more meaningful relationships.

Sociologist Robert S. Weiss refers to this as the "recovery stage" in *Marital Separation*. Having gone through the initial stage of "transition," the person begins to establish a coherent and stable identity with commitments, goals, and values that remain consistent over a period of time and are sensible in terms of the hoped-for future. Moreover, the person develops a stable life pattern, a way of organizing relationships with others that is adequate enough to be self-sustaining.

Sara, who had once identified herself as "a wife" and then as "a mother," now identified herself primarily through her accomplishments at work. She wanted to advance in her career and, at the same time, begin to work toward a more satisfying personal life.

Shortly after moving into her new townhouse, Sara started entertaining a few friends for dinner occasionally. During her married years, she realized, she had spent a lot of time with people she didn't particularly like. She had been meticulous about "repaying" invitations, and her guest lists had often been planned with Jim's business interests in mind. Now, Sara concluded, spending any time with people she didn't like was a waste of time.

Sara said she was open to the idea of remarriage if she should meet the right man. But she accepted the fact that the odds appeared to be against remarriage at her age. She was almost fifty.

Women in the twenty to twenty-four age group have about the same chance of remarriage as men, census figures show. Beyond that age, the possibility decreases every year. By age sixty, there are only twenty-seven available men to one hundred available single women.

The chances of an older woman remarrying are further reduced by the fact that men usually marry women younger than themselves. Although that pattern is gradually changing, women who marry younger men are still in the minority.

THE NEW LAURA

Almost four years had passed since her husband, David, had died, and Laura Cunningham felt comfortable with her "singleness."

Laura had changed in many ways. Although still full-figured, she had lost weight as a result of her exercise class. She had started wearing her hair in a more becoming, shorter style, swept back from her face. She had bought some new clothes, softer and more feminine styles than she'd once worn.

Beyond the physical changes, Laura had acquired a demeanor of self-confidence, an inner glow.

However, many of her old friends and her daughter Anne found the "new Laura" disconcerting. Anne thought her mother should "act her age."

But Laura's friends at the store were complimentary, and Bart's approving glances said more than words.

Laura's decision to have a sexual relationship with Bart became the next milestone in her exploration of life. She rehearsed subtle ways to let him know, but in the end, she was quite direct.

"Would you like to spend the night here?"

They were sitting on the living room couch having coffee and talking at the end of a pleasant evening.

"Yes, I'd like that," Bart said, obviously surprised.

Laura shut herself in the bathroom. She leaned against the sink and took several deep breaths, trying to stop her heart from pounding at the thought of Bart waiting for her, perhaps already in her bed.

Now she had done it! There was no turning back.

Laura slipped a sheer, peach-colored nightgown over her head; then, looking at herself in the bathroom mirror, she fluffed up her hair.

She had thought this out and she wanted to do it, but Bart

had a crude streak that scared her sometimes. What if he expected something out of the ordinary? What if he expected oral sex, a variation she had heard about but had never tried? What if he did something kinky? How would she handle it?

Laura took another deep breath, then opened the door . . . and was stunned by the sight. Bart lay spread out on his back in the middle of her bed wearing nothing except a pair of white boxer shorts. Black, curly hair covered his barrel chest, his stout legs, and even, she noticed with amazement, the tops of his shoulders. She had never seen so much hair.

"Come here," Bart said, holding out his arms.

Laura walked slowly toward the bed and climbed in beside him, reaching for the comforter at the end of the bed.

"We don't need that," Bart said. "I want to see you."

Laura began to suspect she was in for something new. Sex with David had always been a mutual, loving act. David had been gentle and protective. They had made love about twice a month, on a weekend, in the conventional missionary position with the lights off.

Laura wasn't remembering the past. Bart had pulled her close and was running his lips across her eyelids, flicking his tongue across her earlobes, pressing his lips gently but firmly against her mouth. Laura rubbed her hand over his hairy chest, experimentally. As his hand found the nipple of her full breast, Laura trembled slightly and felt a rush of warmth between her legs. She opened her mouth slightly and pushed her body against him. As Bart kissed, gently nibbling her neck, her breasts, her stomach, Laura's breathing came in gasps. She was mesmerized.

As Bart's kisses reached her thighs, Laura parted her legs, startled by the reflex reaction. After the climax came, Laura drew back, but Bart gently persisted, bringing her to the peak of passion three times before resting his face against her leg. And all these years she had thought a climax was singular.

"I love your ass," Bart said, jolting Laura back to reality.

"Come here," she said with a little laugh.

As Bart rose to his knees, his bulging white shorts gave her confidence. She ran her fingers along the elastic band of his shorts and pulled slowly. As she pushed her lover back on the bed, Laura wasn't concerned about her ability to please him. Desire more than compensated for her lack of practice.

It was a night of discovery and mutual pleasure.

Laura was awakened by Bart's steady snoring. Carefully she raised up on her elbow, resting her head on her hand. Bart had a mole on his neck. The hairs in his nose blew back and forth in cadence with his heavy breathing. His stomach, pale and flaccid, rose and fell. Where had he learned how to please, how to bring her to such heights of excitement?

As she studied him, Bart opened his eyes, blinking questioningly.

"Good morning," Laura said, smiling.

Laura's growing self-confidence, her feeling of contentment, had little to do with the circumstances in her life at that time. Her job at the department store was beginning to get boring. Her old house was falling apart. Marcie's college tuition rose every year.

The changes, Laura was realizing, were from within. She was beginning to accept herself as a person, even like herself.

"Let's not spoil it," she said when Bart brought up the subject of marriage.

Laura knew the relationship with Bart was good for her. She enjoyed being with him. She liked looking into his eyes and seeing a nice reflection of herself. She also knew how easy it would be to mistake those feelings for love.

MUTUAL NEEDINESS

Laura was wise to be wary. Since nothing boosts a battered self-esteem as quickly as a new relationship, it's easy to translate any warm, positive feelings into love.

Frank Gardener remarried within a year after his wife, Jill, left him for his best friend, and he knew almost immediately he'd made a mistake.

"I married the first woman I felt comfortable with," Frank said.

His few counseling sessions had at least helped Frank accept the fact that his marriage to Jill was over. Writing in his journal had helped him express some of his grief and anger. Despite these first tentative steps toward recovery, Frank still felt isolated and lonely. The small apartment was depressing. He seldom saw his children. His life seemed to be on a downward spiral.

In this vulnerable state, Frank met Sybil Newman during a two-day trip to the company branch in Columbus, Ohio. A business associate had invited Frank to dinner at his home, and Sybil was among the guests.

As it turned out, Sybil had recently gone through a divorce herself, and she genuinely seemed to understand and empathize with Frank's problems.

A small-boned woman with curly brown hair, her eyes in a constant expression of wonderment, Sybil had a fragile quality about her that made Frank feel strong for the first time in his life. He called her the following morning and asked her out to dinner.

"I feel safe with you," Sybil told Frank that evening as they lingered over dinner in a neighborhood Italian restaurant.

Frank had to tear himself away. He had a full schedule of appointments, with stops at several company branches over the next several weeks. He called Sybil every night.

Frank asked Sybil to meet him in Chicago about a month later, and they crammed their courtship into one long weekend. They talked incessantly about their problems and hopes for the future. They went to bed late, exhausted and happy, in separate rooms. Frank had been sexually passive ever since his divorce. When he'd made the obligatory advances, Sybil had demurely rejected him, only adding to the illusion of her sweetness and purity. On Sunday night, Frank proposed.

Frank got his first clue of problems to come when he met Sybil's mother at their wedding dinner. A domineering woman with a raspy voice, Marie Atwood could not have been more unlike her daughter. In fact, in Marie's presence, Sybil cowered.

"Marie ran our lives," Frank said. "Sybil couldn't buy a curtain without talking to her. Marie picked out the apartment. She picked out furniture. She even told me Sybil wasn't strong enough to have children."

The chances that they would have children were almost nil. Sybil was prone to vague ailments that seemed to coincide with Frank's interest in sex. Frank began referring to her complaints, with some sarcasm, as "the vapors."

Sybil couldn't resist buying new clothes and expensive jars of creams and makeup. Frank accused her of reckless spending, launching their first arguments.

About a year after they were married, Frank came home from a business trip and found Sybil and Marie sitting in the living room. He sensed, correctly, that they were waiting for him. From their grim expressions, Frank knew something was up.

"I think we have a problem," Marie said in her typically brusque manner.

Frank looked at Sybil. She was completely mute.

"By the time we got through, Marie was yelling at me," Frank said later. "She told me I had mistreated her daughter and she wasn't going to put up with it any longer. She ordered me to leave."

Frank packed his bags and left that night. He was relieved, almost eager to leave. At the same time, he felt a deep sense of remorse. Why did his life keep falling apart?

Frank checked in at a downtown hotel. He stopped in the bar and ordered a straight shot of tequila. He drained the glass without stopping, feeling the welcome warmth spread through his body.

Back upstairs in his room, Frank loosened his tie and relaxed in the single upholstered chair. The marriage to Sybil had been a mistake from the beginning: he knew that. As much as he disliked Marie, he knew she had merely been the catalyst that ended it.

Frank also knew he had to find something, to get a grip on his life. As he sat there thinking, a news flash interrupted the music on the radio.

"John Lennon has been shot outside his New York apartment. Please stay tuned for further details."

Frank couldn't believe the awful news. Random violence. He turned the volume up, listening as he got ready for bed. He turned off the light, still listening to the sketchy details of the shooting. He lay there, unable to sleep, until finally he switched on the light and went over to the desk. He found some hotel stationery in the drawer. He spent the next hour writing a short letter to Lennon's wife, Yoko Ono, pausing thoughtfully between sentences.

Frank read the letter over. Actually, he was learning to express himself fairly well, he thought. He sealed the letter, hoping the words would console her in some way if, in fact, they ever reached her. He felt better for having written the letter.

Often, the widowed and divorced remarry too quickly and for the wrong reasons. Rather than make the difficult adjustment to self-reliance, women seek the security of marriage and men seek companionship. In Frank's case, the prognosis for the second marriage wasn't much better than that of the first. He and Sybil came together out of mutual need, too emotionally starved to contribute toward a strong marital relationship.

On the other hand, the best marriages can be second marriages if both partners have swept away the debris from the past and fully achieved independence.

The Reverend Richard L. Kesel, a Presbyterian minister who advises couples considering marriage, sees the positive aspects of second marriages.

"Couples go into their first marriage with starry eyes. They're in love and it's hard for them to believe they're going to have the same problems other people do."

But, he adds, "Couples who come in for counseling before a second marriage have their feet on the ground. They've been through it and they know what can happen. They want the marriage to work out, and they're less self-centered, more concerned about the other person."

Judy Carpenter expressed this unselfish concern when writer Lyle Harrington proposed marriage.

REMARRIAGE—A NEW LIFE

Judy had been sober for more than a year when she met Lyle through her work at the publishing company. A man in his mid-forties, Lyle was putting together a series of his travel articles for a book.

"This time I'm sure it's the real thing," Judy said, arching an eyebrow and smiling at the private joke on herself. "Maybe that's why I have to take some time. I have to be sure I can stay sober. I wouldn't want to put Lyle through the hell of being married to a drinking alcoholic."

Lyle had traveled all over the world on writing assignments, primarily for magazines. The rigors of outdoor life had contributed to his trim, athletic build and his permanently sunburned complexion.

Lyle's first wife had died of a tropical disease while accompanying him on a writing assignment in Africa. It had happened within a year after they'd been married. She had been twenty-three years old at the time and pregnant with their first child. The baby had been stillborn a few weeks before his wife had gone into a coma. A man of deep religious faith, Lyle had found it difficult to accept his loss as God's plan. He had never considered remarriage until he'd met Judy.

Judy not only admired Lyle for his strong faith, maturity, and intelligence, she basked in his circle of literary friends. In a sense, Judy resumed the supportive role she had enjoyed as a faculty wife in Boulder.

"I'm not liberated and I don't want to be," Judy had told Lyle one evening shortly after they'd met. "I don't think it's a question of being equal. Men and women are different, and that has to be for a reason. Why can't they complement each other instead of competing?"

Lyle agreed. He had often had difficulty dealing with assertive women when he returned to the United States after working in other countries. In Judy, Lyle saw a woman who still believed in basic values, a woman who trusted people and life despite all that had happened to her.

Judy had told Lyle about the breakup of her marriage and her struggle with alcoholism, but, afraid of hurting him, she had spared him details about other men.

"Thanks to God and A.A., I'm overcoming it," she told him. "But it's still a day at a time."

Lyle proposed marriage at the end of their first summer together. He was leaving for an assignment in London and wanted to announce their engagement to their friends before he left.

"Believe me, I want to shout it from the rooftops," Judy said. "But we've got to be sure."

They agreed to postpone the wedding until the following summer.

"We talked about living together before we got married, but neither one of us felt comfortable with it," Judy said. "I don't call myself a born-again Christian, but the fact is, my life wasn't going very well until I put my trust in God."

Judy and Lyle were married the following August in a small chapel in New York City. Only a few of the guests knew they were celebrating Judy's sobriety as well as the marriage of their good friends.

Judy looked radiant in a pastel-pink gown with a single strand of pearls that Lyle had given her as a wedding gift. Kristen and Lyle's brother were the only attendants.

They spent a month in Germany, where Lyle had a freelance writing assignment.

"Kristen will be going away to college before long," Judy had said. "We'd like to start over and have a family, but if we can't have children of our own, we'll adopt."

Roughly nine months later, Judy sent out birth announcements.

SETTING PRIORITIES

Life seemed particularly chaotic to Richard Morrison that morning. Jason was burning the toast to a crisp and insisting he liked his toast dark.

"You're so immature, Jason," Mandy said. "Go wash your face or you'll be late for school."

The washer had broken down and Richard was trying to reach a repairman on the telephone. He still had to finish dressing, and he had an early appointment at the office.

He was being punished, no doubt, for having been such a clod with Gloria the night before, Richard thought grimly. He'd been so sure she would understand why he couldn't think about getting married for some time.

"I've seen what can happen when you try to bring two families together," Richard had said. "Love does not conquer all."

Clearly, Gloria had not understood. In fact, Richard decided, she had misunderstood the whole point. He probably should have spared her the part about "always being good friends." That comment had definitely brought out some hostility.

"You're both going to be late," Richard said firmly, hanging up the telephone. He'd have to try the repairman later in the day.

"Mandy, what's wrong with your hair?"

Mandy was busily putting the breakfast dishes in the dishwasher.

"Nothing's *wrong* with it," she said airily. "It's the style."

Richard couldn't imagine how Mandy had achieved the halo of Orphan Annie curls, but he decided that was another item that could be discussed later. Maybe Gloria would have a word with her. Gloria. Richard sighed as he went upstairs to finish dressing. Gloria might not be so available from now on.

Richard and Gloria had met at a Parents Without Partners meeting, and in a short time she had become a surrogate mother to his children. A divorcée with a daughter Mandy's age, Gloria had helped Mandy shop for clothes and talked to her about the facts of life. Richard was grateful for her help and her friendship. Their children and their own efforts to be good single parents invariably dominated the conversation on their dates. Did he love Gloria? Richard wasn't sure.

Richard wasn't ready to think about love and marriage. The children were beginning to adjust, and he was beginning to set some priorities. The most important, he had decided, was to make a career change. His unpredictable hours as an insurance agent didn't mesh with his new responsibilities as a single parent. And, Richard finally admitted to himself, the work had become less gratifying.

He began to think about his early ambition to become a teacher, plans he had been forced to put aside when Peggy had told him she was pregnant.

A counselor at the local community college encouraged Richard. The credits he had acquired in liberal arts courses during his first year of college were transferable. He could get additional credits for life experiences by passing certain tests.

The counselor suggested Richard apply for a scholarship and financial aid. In subsequent meetings, she helped him work out a class schedule that would enable him to continue working part-time for two years. She suggested he plan ahead so that he could carry a full schedule in his senior year.

"We held a family conference and decided to give it a try," Richard said. "I'm sure it won't be easy, but the kids are as excited about it as I am."

Richard and his children had become "a family" again, with shared plans and goals. They had problems, as all families do, but Richard had stopped trying to replace Peggy and be two parents. He was learning to trust his instincts.

"I'm criticized sometimes for giving the kids too much responsibility," Richard said. "My sister hit the roof when I taught Jason to use the power lawn mower. I spent some time showing him how to use it and I trust him. I'm trying not to worry so much about what other people think."

STARTING OVER

The telephone was ringing, but Carol Dwyer couldn't find the telephone. The painters had shoved all the office furniture into the middle of the room and covered it with a heavy gray tarpaulin.

"Keep ringing!"

Frantically tracking the steady ring, Carol located the telephone in the kneehole of the desk. Lying flat on her stomach, she picked up the receiver. "Dwyer Associates," she said breathlessly.

The name still had a new, wonderful sound to it.

Carol dug into a desk drawer and found a pad and pen. Speaking as naturally as possible under the circumstances, she asked some questions and scribbled some notes. The call was from the public relations manager of an independent television station regarding a publicity campaign. He had hired Carol to do the graphics.

"I'm taking any and all jobs that come along," Carol said, dusting off the front of her bulky-knit red sweater. "Even if they're not creative, they pay the rent."

After the divorce, Carol had gone back to Chicago and tried to resume working with her ex-husband, Bob, and his homosexual lover, Paul. She had thought about it during the months she'd spent on the couple's Bucks County farm.

"I decided the business partnership was all we could salvage from the marriage," Carol said. "But I couldn't handle it. Everything had changed."

As she talked, Carol pushed back the tarpaulin and pulled out some chairs. Carefully she poured two black coffees from a Thermos into Styrofoam cups.

"It took me a long time and a lot of sessions with a therapist to accept the fact that I was clinging to that business because I needed the security," Carol said. "I didn't really believe I could make it on my own."

Carol described two more years of clinging, white-knuckled, to any job that seemed to offer security. She had found a position in the graphics department of a major advertising firm in Chicago. Supposedly hired to do graphics, she'd done everything from making the coffee to escorting visiting celebrities to talk shows. A year later, she had grabbed the offer of a transfer to New York City, but the opportunity for advancement hadn't appeared to be any better. For every opening at the top, there had been ten people fighting tooth and nail.

One morning, stuck in traffic on Madison Avenue, Carol had made a decision. She knew the public relations business.

She had some money saved. She was willing to work hard. She had to start her own business.

"I can't describe the feeling of exhilaration," Carol said of this moment when she'd finally taken stock and decided to go on her own. "I've made a lot of mistakes. I've made dozens of proposals on work I didn't get. Some nights, when I'm here until eleven or twelve, I wonder why I don't give up."

After more than a year, Carol was expanding her office space and hiring a second writer. She'd had stationery and business cards printed with her new official name, Dwyer Associates. She had just submitted a proposal for marketing a series of foreign television films to cable systems in the United States. As she talked about her business, Carol's expression was calm, her eyes steady.

What a contrast to the frightened, fragile woman who had described the breakup of her marriage almost four years ago!

"By the way," Carol said, "the reason I haven't given up is that I've never been this happy."

The telephone was ringing.

In the end, the trauma of becoming "suddenly single" is a personal experience. The feeling of being abandoned, of being totally isolated, overwhelms everything else for a time. Friendships may suddenly seem shallow. Close relatives may appear heartless. Even one's children may temporarily be forgotten. Despair may obliterate simple pleasures.

If personal identity has been closely linked with the marriage, if "the two have become one," as in Sara's and Laura's marriages, the task resembles unscrambling an egg. It involves taking a painstaking inventory of one's strengths and accomplishments, a recentering of one's life.

Progress can be erratic, and some find it easier than others. Furthermore, this new and fragile identity can easily succumb to the fatal attraction of a facile dependence upon another. As Frank learned, remarriage must be carefully considered. One must be ready to give, and strong enough to give. One must be secure enough to put another person's satisfaction on the same level as one's own. As Richard understood, love does not conquer all.

EPILOGUE

The letter from Sara Johnston was postmarked St. Croix, Virgin Islands, and a color photo dropped onto the desk as I unfolded the single sheet of hotel stationery.

The photo was of Sara and a tall, slender man, posing beneath a palm tree. With their deep tans, bikini bathing suits, and smiling faces, the photo could have been featured on a travel brochure.

> My first real vacation in years! Just so you won't think I turned into a complete workaholic, I'm sending the proof. Meet Sean. He's a lab technician at the hospital and a wonderful friend. We moved in together last fall. I couldn't resist his cooking!
>
> Love,
Sara
>
> P.S. Sean is fifteen years younger than me, so I don't want to think about marriage. I never was a trendsetter.

I sat there looking at the photograph, remembering the tense, middle-aged woman I had met for the first time for lunch in New York. The Sara in the photograph looked younger, vibrant.

What had happened to the others? We had spent many hours with each of them, talking about the most intimate details of their lives. Then, having allowed us to know and care about them, they had gone their separate ways—vowing to keep in touch. The note from Sara made us curious.

Laura and Bart were married.

They had the wedding in Laura's living room with only the family and a few close friends present. Anne and her family had been noticeably absent.

"I've asked them to come during the holidays," Laura said. "We'll be in our own house by then. Maybe it won't be so painful for her."

Anne's absence didn't detract from the festive mood. Bart had repainted the house, inside and out, preparing to put it up for sale. Laura had made loose bouquets of garden flowers throughout the house. Greta and Marcie prepared a festive wedding luncheon.

"There may be snow on the roof, but there's still a fire in the furnace," Bart said, lifting his champagne glass to his bride.

Laura smiled tolerantly.

Richard Morrison was teaching high school.

Richard's graduation from college had been a major family event. His parents had come from out of town. Mandy and Jason were there, of course, and so were Gloria and her daughter.

Gloria had surprised Richard. Although they had stopped dating each other exclusively, they had remained friends. Gloria had been helpful and supportive when Richard had the burden of managing the house, working part-time, and going to school.

"This is your day, too," Richard told Gloria, insisting she join the family for a celebratory dinner out.

Debbie Matheson had remarried.

"You should be writing a book on two-career families," Debbie said. "Bill's company just offered him a promotion and it means moving to San Francisco. It's too good to pass up, so I'm going to be job hunting. I suppose we'll be facing those decisions from now on. And somewhere along the line, we want to start a family."

Debbie said her divorce didn't make her more cautious the second time, but she is more willing to talk and try to work things out.

"I've discovered men have certain traits and you can't change that," Debbie said. "It's amazing. I wish I'd known that the first time."

Carol Dwyer was still putting long hours into her public relations business.

"I'm dating a special friend, and we plan to get married someday," Carol said. "I guess the most encouraging development is that Bob and I are friends again. We keep in touch professionally. That's been good."

Judy, Lyle, and their son were living in Wales.

"We've decided to settle down now that Eric's in school," Judy wrote. "Lyle is working on another book. I bake bread and we raise most of our vegetables. You wouldn't recognize me!"

Judy said Kristen still spent her summers with Stephen and

his wife in Boulder but usually spent her long midsemester holiday with Judy and Lyle in Wales.

"Kristen has made the dean's list every semester, and she's really a responsible young woman. When I think of how much I used to worry about her!"

Mark Trowbridge no longer said, "My work is my life."
Work was still an important part of his life, but now he looked forward to spending his vacations and most of his free time with Jennifer.

Mark said he was changing his priorities and learning to relax more. He thought he might take early retirement and spend some time traveling. He and Jennifer had talked about getting married or living together, but so far they were satisfied with things as they were.

"We don't see any reason to make a change," Mark said. "Jenny has her life and I have mine. Marriage might be a consideration at some point."

Frank Gardener, certainly the most vulnerable at our last meeting, was the most difficult to locate. He had changed jobs and moved.

"I'm working on the basics," Frank said with a laugh, explaining he had decided his children needed to be given priority. They were growing up and hardly knew him.

Frank had moved to a position with a small company that didn't require traveling. He had bought an older duplex house in an urban-renewal area and was working on the renovations himself.

"I see the kids every other weekend and most holidays," Frank said. "Jill is a little easier to get along with now that I'm keeping up the support payments and have settled down."

The renovations on the house had been a major project.

Frank had spent hours sanding old moldings, ripping out plumbing, and learning how to install drywall. As the house improved, so did the repairs to his psyche.

"I won't say I'll never marry again," Frank said thoughtfully. "I will say I won't marry again until I'm ready."

From those who had remarried and those who had not, we discovered a fundamental truth: A person must accept the fact that loneliness doesn't come from being alone, after all, but from dissatisfaction with oneself.

To the person who is still grieving, the task of "working through" may seem almost impossible. Of those who shared their stories with us, the more successful showed that the task is not only possible, but worth the effort, however long it takes. In retrospect, they believe now that their burden would have been lightened if they had known their feelings were quite normal, and if they had known there was hope.

With time and the help of loving friends and, perhaps, some professional direction or extra strength derived from belief in God, the deep wound will heal from the inside out. One must walk, talk, and try, until the lost loved one has not only been put to rest, but has been replaced by one's own new self-realization. From that comes the freedom to live fully in the present and look forward to the future, with others no less than oneself.

That is the ultimate key to overcoming adversity—the willingness to put your best into today and prepare to move gracefully into tomorrow.

FOR FURTHER READING

Bolles, Richard Nelson. *What Color Is Your Parachute?* Berkeley, Calif.: Ten Speed Press, 1982. A popular guide to job hunting and career changing. The author explains why traditional methods of job hunting don't work and offers detailed, innovative approaches. An optimistic view of the workplace that should encourage anyone who is looking for a job or seeking a career change.

Brothers, Joyce. *What Every Woman Should Know About Men.* New York: Ballantine Books, 1981. An entertaining look at male development with explanations for why men behave the way they do. The author offers answers to the most puzzling questions about men—from why they value their jobs above everything to why they leave the toilet seat up. A helpful book for women who want to improve their relationships with men.

Burns, David. *Feeling Good: The New Mood Therapy.* New York: William Morrow & Co., 1980. A simple explanation of cognitive therapy and how it can be applied by the layman. Among the pioneers in the field of cognitive therapy, Dr. Burns contends that moods can be changed by altering the way one thinks. The step-by-step approach to changing one's thinking patterns should be useful to anyone suffering from negative feelings—anxiety, depression, loss of self-esteem.

Buscaglia, Leo. *Loving Each Other*. New York: Holt, Rinehart & Winston, 1984. A thoughtful exploration of relationships, including the results of a survey on how people feel about their primary relationships. The author believes people have a need to relate to each other, but social attitudes tend to discourage the fulfillment of this basic need. By exploring such questions as how we define love and friendship, the author sheds light on the meaning of relationships and offers suggestions on improving the way we relate to each other.

Caine, Lynn. *Lifelines*. New York: Doubleday & Co., 1978. In this sequel to her personal memoir, *Widow*, the author describes her efforts to find fulfillment as a single woman. The candid accounts of her personal experiences, interspersed with practical advice, should be helpful to women who are attempting to rebuild their lives after the loss of a loved one.

Colgrove, Melba, Bloomfield, Harold H., & McWilliams, Peter. *How to Survive the Loss of a Love*. New York: Bantam Books, 1979. A small book of poetry and inspirational reading that addresses all types of loss. A natural for the night table.

Dowling, Colette. *The Cinderella Complex*. New York: Summit Books, 1982. An in-depth exploration into why women fear independence. The author's personal experiences and case histories provide insight on how this pattern of dependence can slowly be changed. An encouraging book for any woman who fears being alone.

Dyer, Wayne W. *Your Erroneous Zones*. New York: Avon Books, 1977. A how-to book on breaking free of the past, ridding oneself of useless emotions, and beginning to take greater control of one's life.

———. *Pulling Your Own Strings*. New York: Avon Books, 1979. A follow-up to *Your Erroneous Zones*, in which the author shows how to be more assertive, though not necessarily aggressive, in dealing with others. The books should be helpful to anyone who feels "victimized" or stuck with useless emotions such as guilt.

Ellis, Albert, & Harper, R. A. *A New Guide to Rational Living*. North Hollywood, Calif.: Wilshire Book Co., 1975. A self-help book describing rational emotive psychotherapy. The authors describe how emotional problems can be solved through modifying the thinking process.

Emery, G. A. *A New Beginning*. New York: Simon & Schuster, 1981. The author explains the principles of cognitive therapy and how to apply the concept in a treatment of depression.

Fisher, Bruce. *Rebuilding*. San Luis Obispo, Calif.: Impact Publishers, 1983. The author uses symbolic "building blocks" to illustrate the grief stages following the end of a love relationship and a symbolic mountain to illustrate the struggle to reach the peak stage of "singleness" and independence. The sympathetic, personal approach seems simplistic, but in many cases, this is exactly what the grieving person needs. Much of the material came from the author's "Divorce and Personal Growth" seminars.

Fonda, Jane. *Women Coming of Age*. New York: Simon & Schuster, 1984. The author, in noticeably good shape herself, explains what happens to the body at middle age and offers suggestions for a healthy life-style that would probably be beneficial at any age. While most of the information on diet and exercise is available elsewhere, it's helpful to have it all in one place. The tone of the book is helpful, even sympathetic, to human weaknesses, unlike the intimidating style of many health books.

Forbes, Rosalind. *Life Stress*. New York: Doubleday & Co., 1979. The book covers some of the most common sources of daily stress along with helpful advice on how to identify and reduce stress. Although she sometimes fails to make the distinction between stress and distress in the early chapters, the author includes a discussion on positive stress and how it can be used to enhance social, work, and home situations. A simple, nontechnical book for people who may be feeling somewhat overwhelmed by life.

Friedman, James T. *The Divorce Handbook*. New York: Random House, 1984. The legal aspects of divorce are thoroughly covered in question-answer form, with worksheets and checklists that should simplify the divorce process to a person facing the legal maze for the first time. While covering major issues such as child custody, the author also answers many questions the client would probably never think to ask, such as how to dress for a court appearance.

Gardner, Richard. *The Boys and Girls Book About Divorce.* New York: Science House, 1970. Written for children at the junior high level, this book discusses divorce from the child's point of view. A good one for parents and children to read together, particularly if the children seem to be having difficulty expressing their feelings about their parents' divorce.

Hafer, W. Keith. *Coping with Bereavement from Death Or Divorce.* Englewood Cliffs, N.J.: Prentice-Hall, 1981. Written by a marriage and family counselor, this small book provides a simple, detailed explanation of the grief process with suggestions on how the bereaved person can cope and overcome grief. A section on the bereaved child includes possible behavioral changes to watch for and how to help a child express grief.

Hansen, James C. *Death and Grief in the Family.* Rockville, Md.: Aspen, 1984. Contributing editors discuss various aspects of grief and coping devices. Written primarily for family therapists and other professionals.

Harris, Thomas. *I'm OK—You're OK.* New York: Avon Books, 1973. A popular book on transactional analysis, based in part on the premise that how we feel about ourselves influences our relationships with others. The book is not light reading but should be helpful to anyone seeking greater self-understanding.

Hoffer, Eric. *The Ordeal of Change.* New York: Harper & Row, 1963. A collection of essays on change from the personal to the national level. A thoughtful book for those interested in exploring change on a philosophical level.

Kaplan, Peter W. *Single States, a Total Guide to the State of Being Alone.* New York: Ballantine Books, 1983. An irreverent look at single life, including a tour of major cities as viewed primarily from the singles bar. Only for people who are ready to laugh at their "single state."

Kliman, Ann S. *Crisis, Psychological First Aid for Recovery and*

Growth. New York: Holt, Rinehart & Winston, 1978. Based on her work in crisis intervention, the author uses case histories to illustrate immediate measures that can be taken to help individuals and families survive a personal tragedy. Case histories reveal the varied, normal reactions to grief and the process of working through to recovery.

Krantzler, Melvin. *Creative Divorce*. New York: M. Evans, 1974. A best-selling book on how to turn a divorce into a creative experience.

———. *Learning to Love Again*. New York: Bantam Books, 1979. Using his personal experiences and case histories, the author describes how to let go of old ways and establish new relationships.

List, Julie Autumn. *The Day the Loving Stopped*. New York: Seaview, 1980. A first-person account of divorce from a child's point of view. The author was nine years old when her father moved out of the house. Shortly after, she started the journal that provides the background for this book, along with the letters she wrote to her father.

Newman, Mildred, & Berkowitz, Bernard. *How to Be Your Own Best Friend*. New York: Ballantine Books, 1983. A conversation with two psychoanalysts on mastering the art of being happy. An inspirational little book to carry around.

Robertson, Christina. *Divorce and Decision Making, a Woman's Guide*. Chicago: Follett Publishing Co., 1980. A well-organized, thorough coverage of the special problems confronting the divorced woman. The author first addresses such topics as support systems and values, then turns her attention to specific decisions that have to be made.

Rogers, Carl. *Becoming Partners*. New York: Dell Publishing Co., 1972. Interviews with couples from a variety of life-styles. A helpful book for anyone interested in developing lasting relationships.

Salk, Lee. *What Every Child Would Like Parents to Know About Divorce*. New York: Harper & Row, 1978. A child psychologist talks about children of divorce. The book will help divorcing parents who are interested in easing the trauma for their children.

Schuller, Robert H. *Turning Your Stress Into Strength*. New York: Fawcett Books, 1979. In this spiritual approach to dealing with stress, the author advocates conquering stress through faith in God. In the belief that stress caused by personal tragedy, fatigue, illness, and personal failure can be overcome by faith in God, the author illustrates steps to strength and happiness through personal stories of faith.

Selye, Hans. *Stress Without Distress*. New York: Signet, 1975. The dean of stress researchers insists that stress can be the spice of life. In this uplifting book, the author explains the psychological mechanism of stress and how it can be used to enhance one's life, turning work into joyful play.

Sheehy, Gail. *Pathfinders*. New York: Bantam Books, 1981. A well-researched book about people who have overcome adversity, "life accidents," and the qualities that appear to set them apart.

Silverstone, Barbara, & Hyman, Helen Kandel. *You and Your Aging Parent*. New York: Pantheon Books, 1976. The authors take an in-depth look at the problems adult children and their aging parents face, including the emotional, physical, and financial aspects. They have approached a difficult topic with sympathy and compassion for both child and parent, admitting there are no pat answers.

Tatebaum, Judy. *The Courage to Grieve*. New York: Harper & Row, 1970. Following the death of her brother in 1956, the author went into a lengthy mourning period. Finally helped by Gestalt therapy in 1970, she became interested in helping others deal with grief. She describes the stages of mourning and suggests ways in which people can prepare themselves to deal with death.

Toffler, A. *Future Shock*. New York: Random House, 1970. A popular book about the constant changes in society and how people adapt to the future.

Troyer, Warner. *Divorced Kids*. New York: Harcourt Brace Jovanovich, 1980. Revealing interviews with children of divorced parents. Children between the ages of five and fifteen, plus a few adults who recall their experiences, talk about everything from money problems to their parents' new lovers.

The book is an eye-opener for parents at any stage of divorce.

Weekes, Claire. *Simple, Effective Treatment of Agoraphobia.* New York: Bantam Books, 1981. A pioneer in the study of nervous illness, Dr. Weekes explains the causes for the anxiety state produced by fear of crowds and open spaces. Her step-by-step treatment for overcoming agoraphobia is based on reducing tension by understanding and acceptance. Written primarily for therapists and practitioners, the book is often recommended to patients to help them understand the anxiety state.

Weiss, Robert S. *Marital Separation.* New York: Basic Books, 1975. Using case histories from his "Seminars for the Separated," the author addresses the many aspects of separation trauma and loss. Dr. Weiss offers explanations for the varied reactions to loss and suggestions on how to deal with the myriad of feelings. He goes on to describe the period of starting over, dating, and forming new attachments.

Wheeler, Michael. *Divided Children.* New York: W. W. Norton & Co., 1980. An informative book about the legal aspects of divorce as they apply to children. In addition to the obvious questions of custody and child support, the author covers such areas as grandparents' rights and ownership of property.

Wilkie, Jane. *The Divorced Woman's Handbook.* New York: William Morrow & Co., 1980. The author focuses on the divorced woman's first year alone, offering practical advice on such matters as finances, how to change one's name, health, children, work, social life, and moving.